JUMBLE

TIME MACHINE: 1972

A collection of puzzles from 50 years ago!

Henri Arnold,
Bob Lee,
David L. Hoyt
and Jeff Knurek

TRIUMPH
BOOKS

This book is available in quantity at special discounts
for your group or organization.

For further information, contact:
Triumph Books LLC
814 North Franklin Street
Chicago, Illinois 60610
Phone: (312) 337-0747
www.triumphbooks.com

Printed in U.S.A.

ISBN: 978-1-63727-082-0

Design by Sue Knopf

Contents

JUMBLE
TIME MACHINE: 1972

Classic Puzzles

1972
PUZZLE
1

JUMBLE®

Unscramble these four Jumbles, one letter to each square, to form four ordinary words.

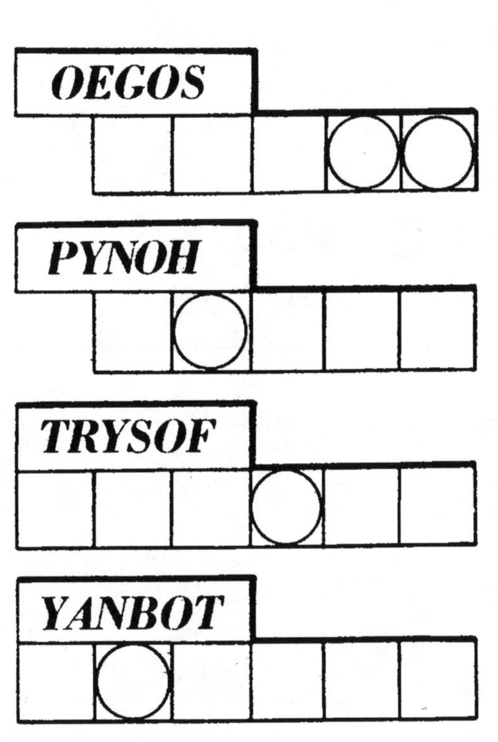
OEGOS
PYNOH
TRYSOF
YANBOT

I'm right!
DRUGS
No, I'm right!
ODD IF THEY'RE BOTH RIGHT!

Now arrange the circled letters to form the surprise answer, as suggested by the above cartoon.

Print answer here 

1972
PUZZLE
2

JUMBLE®

Unscramble these four Jumbles, one letter to each square, to form four ordinary words.

OPTIV

MOURF

TANDLE

AMIDDY

Hi, baby!

RESTAURA

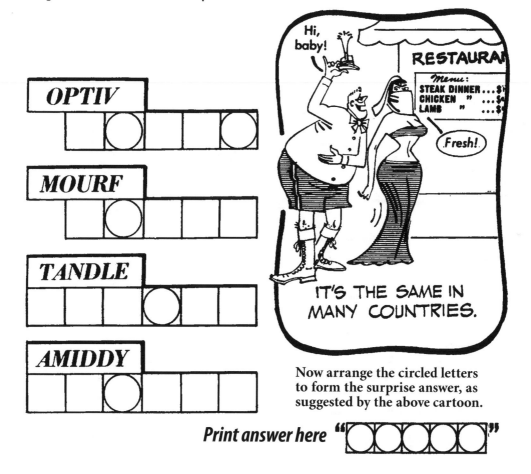

Menu:
STEAK DINNER...
CHICKEN " ...
LAMB " ...

Fresh!

IT'S THE SAME IN MANY COUNTRIES.

Now arrange the circled letters to form the surprise answer, as suggested by the above cartoon.

Print answer here " "

1972
PUZZLE
3

JUMBLE®

Unscramble these four Jumbles, one letter to each square, to form four ordinary words.

DOORE

NOAPI

SCIBEP

ENMIRE

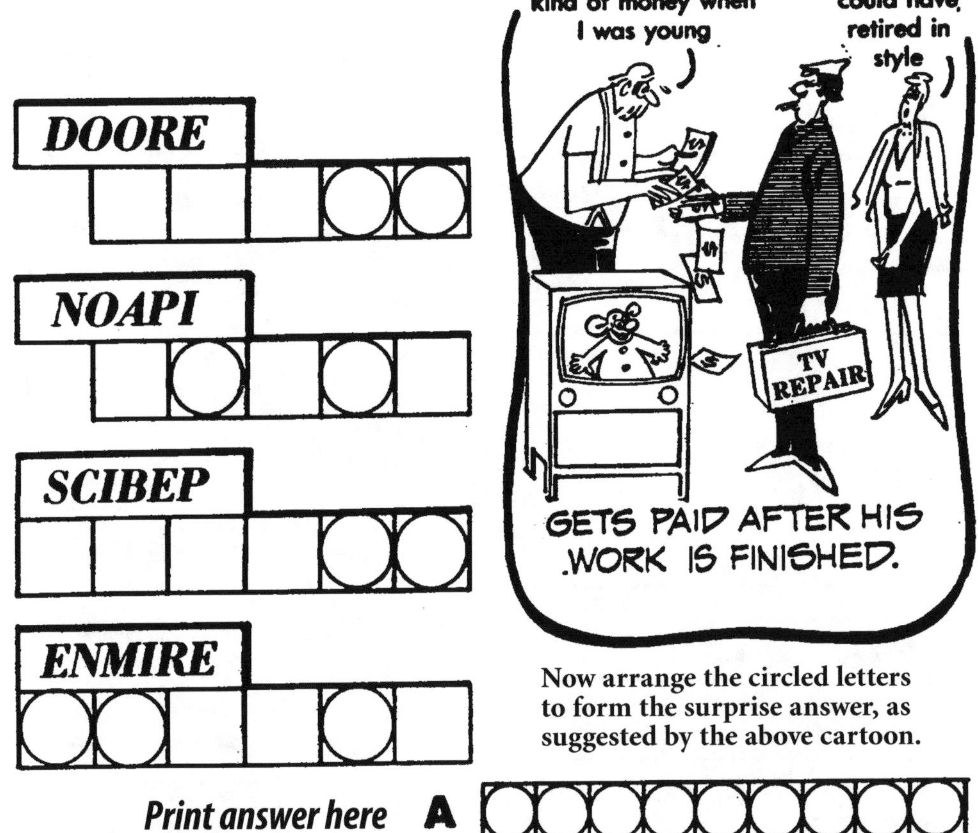
Wish I'd made this kind of money when I was young
Then we could have retired in style
TV REPAIR
GETS PAID AFTER HIS WORK IS FINISHED.

Now arrange the circled letters to form the surprise answer, as suggested by the above cartoon.

Print answer here A

1972
PUZZLE
4

JUMBLE®

Unscramble these four Jumbles, one letter to each square, to form four ordinary words.

DONUP

POURC

LAUMSY

SHOPIN

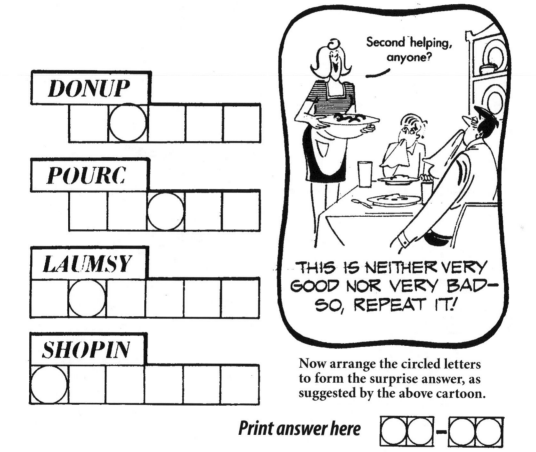

Second helping, anyone?

THIS IS NEITHER VERY GOOD NOR VERY BAD— SO, REPEAT IT!

Now arrange the circled letters to form the surprise answer, as suggested by the above cartoon.

Print answer here ☐☐-☐☐

1972
PUZZLE
5

JUMBLE®

Unscramble these four Jumbles, one letter to each square, to form four ordinary words.

TOOPH

LIDAY

BELTOT

DRIFOL

WHY THE GUNMAN AND HIS GUN WERE DANGEROUS.

Now arrange the circled letters to form the surprise answer, as suggested by the above cartoon.

Print answer here ◯◯◯◯ WERE ◯◯◯◯◯◯

1972
PUZZLE
6

JUMBLE®

Unscramble these four Jumbles, one letter to each square, to form four ordinary words.

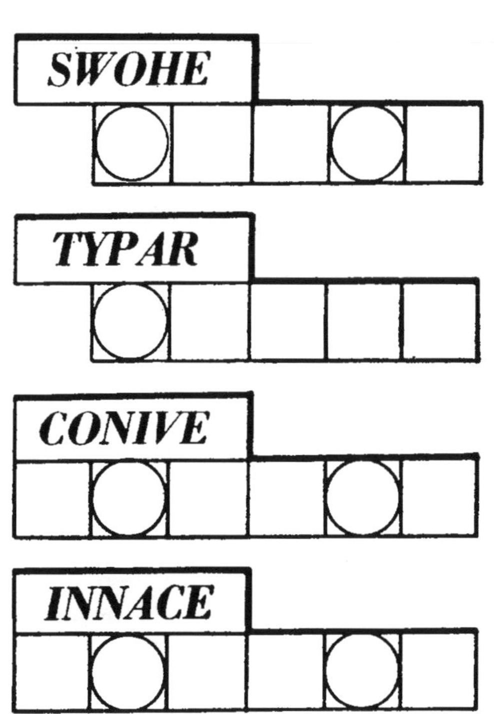

SWOHE
TYPAR
CONIVE
INNACE

BOARD OF DIRECTORS
THIS MIGHT BE RESPONSIBLE FOR A CERTAIN COOLNESS AT THE TOP.

Now arrange the circled letters to form the surprise answer, as suggested by the above cartoon.

Print answer here **A** 

1972
PUZZLE
7

JUMBLE®

Unscramble these four Jumbles, one letter to each square, to form four ordinary words.

DUGEN

YANON

HIRCUN

DILERB

Not tonight—maybe tomorrow
WHAT THE FRUSTRATED RACEHORSE WAS ALWAYS GETTING.

Now arrange the circled letters to form the surprise answer, as suggested by the above cartoon.

Print answer here **THE**

1972
PUZZLE
8

JUMBLE®

Unscramble these four Jumbles, one letter to each square, to form four ordinary words.

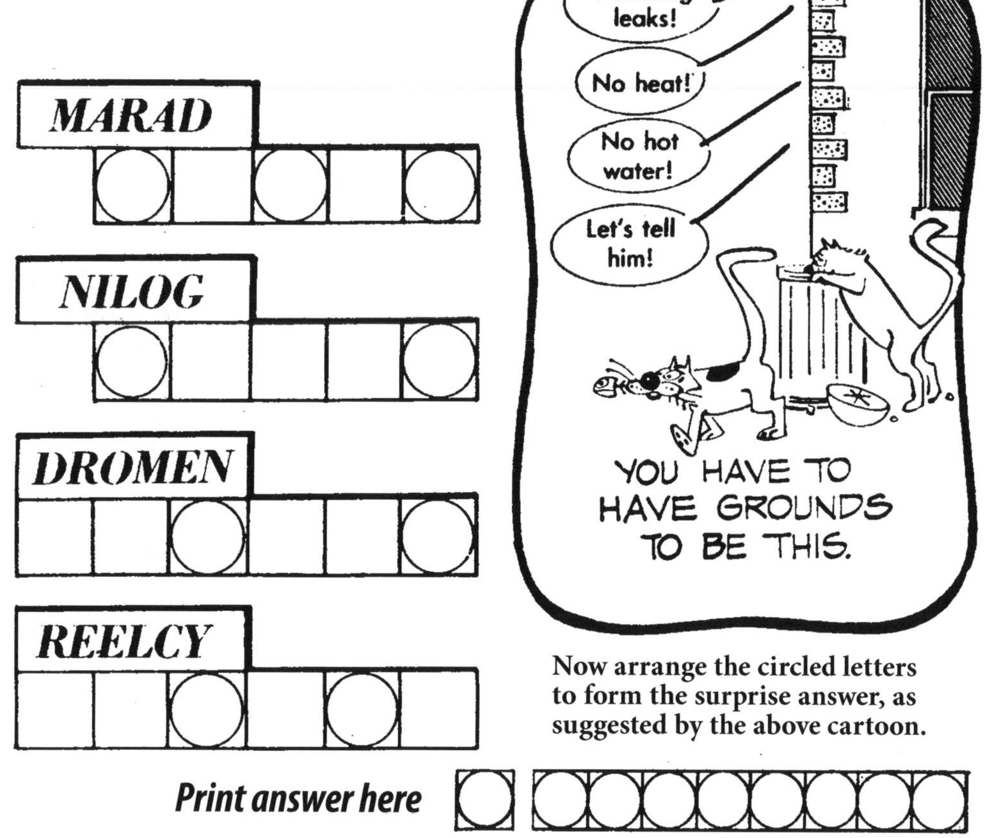
MARAD
NILOG
DROMEN
REELCY
Plumbing leaks!
No heat!
No hot water!
Let's tell him!
YOU HAVE TO HAVE GROUNDS TO BE THIS.

Now arrange the circled letters to form the surprise answer, as suggested by the above cartoon.

Print answer here

1972
PUZZLE
9

JUMBLE®

Unscramble these four Jumbles, one letter to each square, to form four ordinary words.

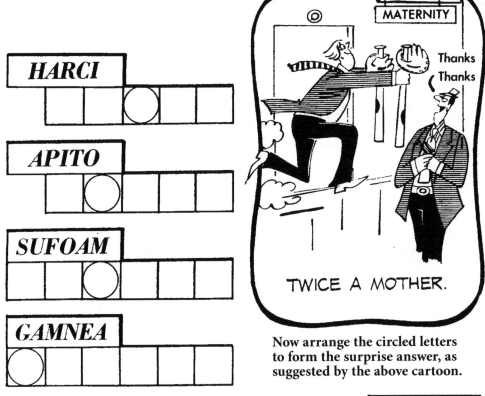

HARCI

APITO

SUFOAM

GAMNEA

MATERNITY

Thanks

Thanks

TWICE A MOTHER.

Now arrange the circled letters to form the surprise answer, as suggested by the above cartoon.

Print answer here

1972
PUZZLE
10

JUMBLE®

Unscramble these four Jumbles, one letter to each square, to form four ordinary words.

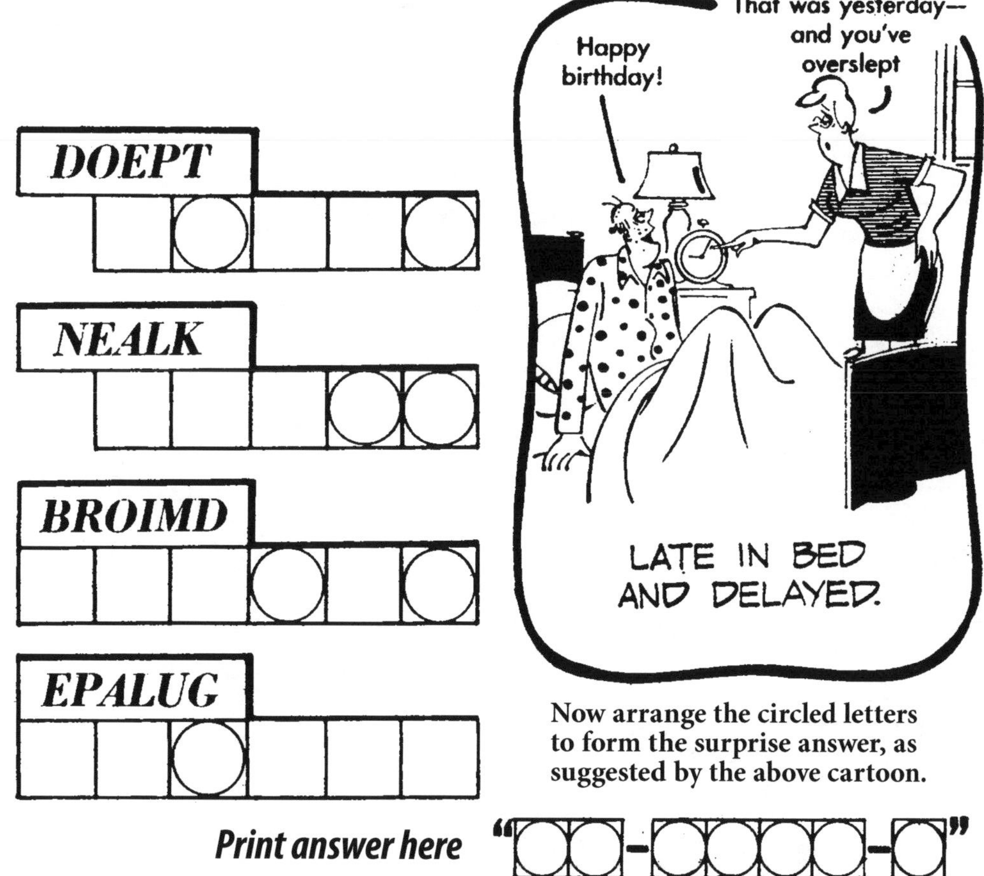
DOEPT
NEALK
BROIMD
EPALUG
Happy birthday!
That was yesterday— and you've overslept
LATE IN BED AND DELAYED.

Now arrange the circled letters to form the surprise answer, as suggested by the above cartoon.

Print answer here "◯◯-◯◯◯◯◯-◯"

1972
PUZZLE
11

JUMBLE®

Unscramble these four Jumbles, one letter to each square, to form four ordinary words.

HIEWL

MOGAD

NICCIP

CHOROB

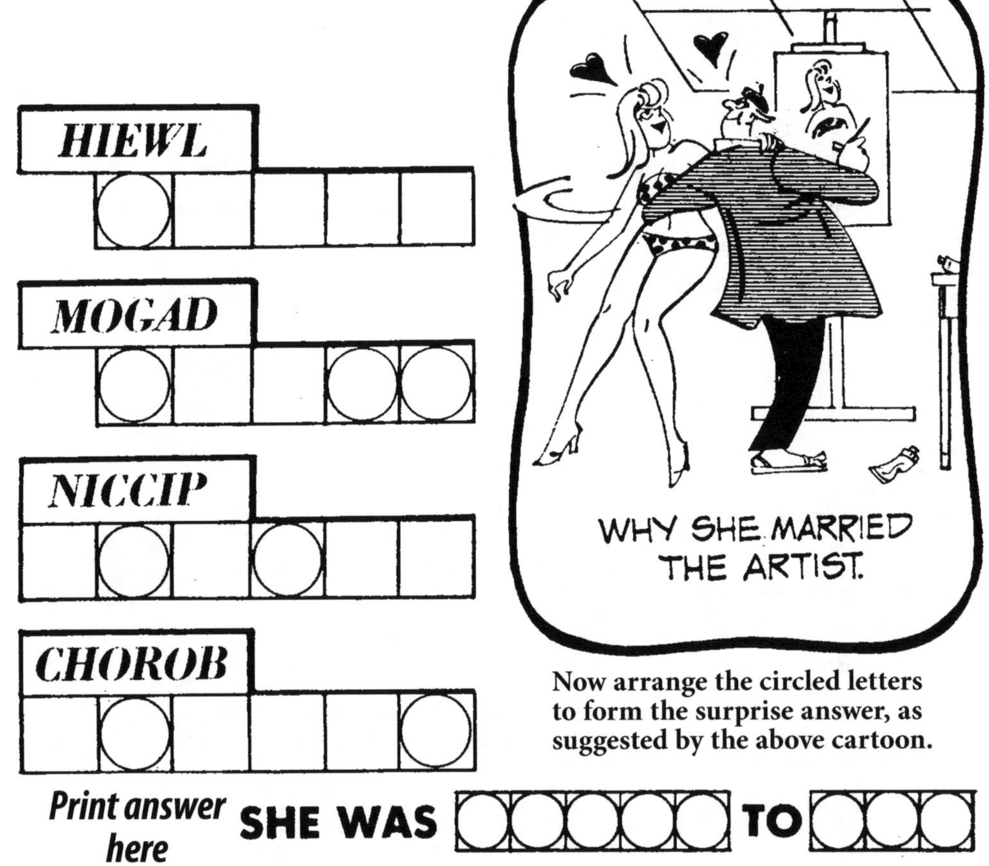
WHY SHE MARRIED THE ARTIST.

Now arrange the circled letters to form the surprise answer, as suggested by the above cartoon.

Print answer here **SHE WAS** ______ **TO** ___

1972
PUZZLE
12

JUMBLE®

Unscramble these four Jumbles, one letter to each square, to form four ordinary words.

FYFAT

DOREL

HUPNAC

ZEBRAL

MUSIC
THIS IS THE RESULT OF A MUSICAL STRIKE.

Now arrange the circled letters to form the surprise answer, as suggested by the above cartoon.

Print answer here

1972
PUZZLE
13

JUMBLE®

Unscramble these four Jumbles, one letter to each square, to form four ordinary words.

UGAVE

LIRLT

TAYFUL

BOICED

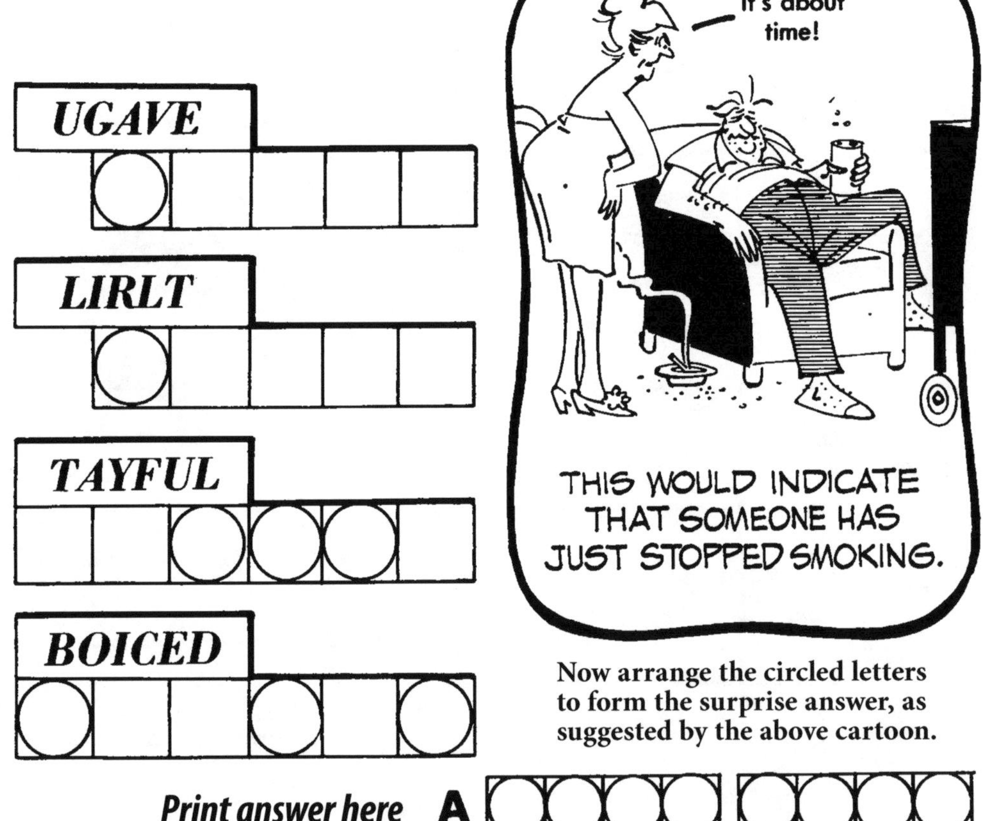
It's about time!
THIS WOULD INDICATE THAT SOMEONE HAS JUST STOPPED SMOKING.

Now arrange the circled letters to form the surprise answer, as suggested by the above cartoon.

Print answer here **A**

1972
PUZZLE
14

JUMBLE®

Unscramble these four Jumbles, one letter to each square, to form four ordinary words.

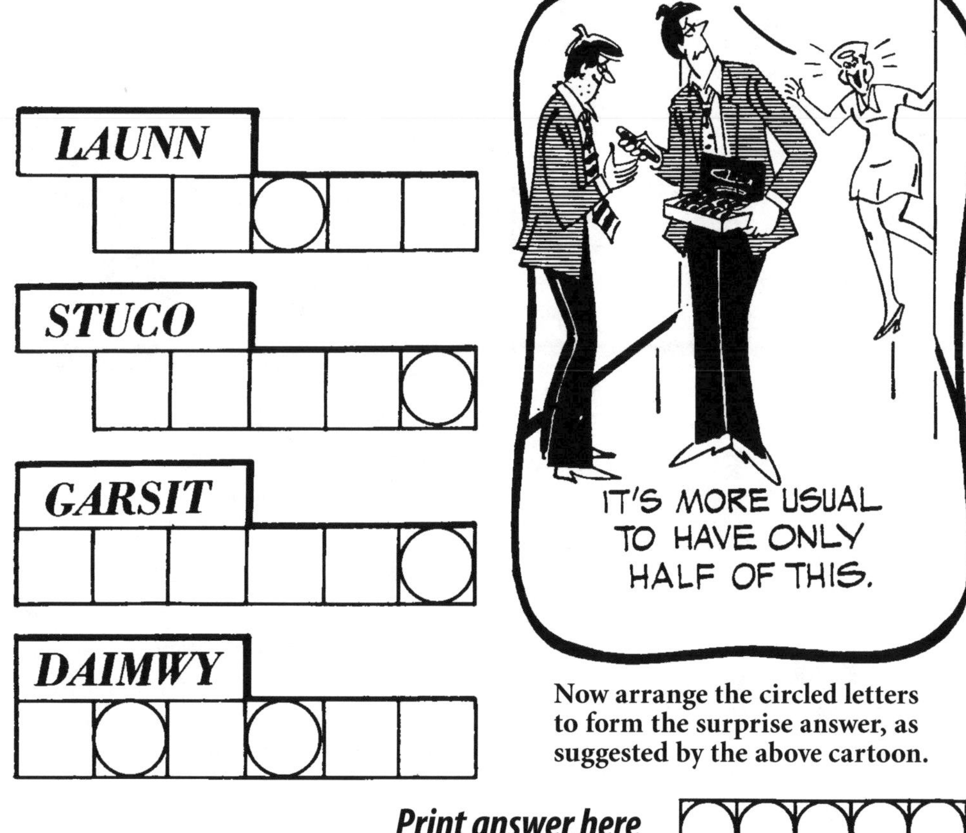
LAUNN
STUCO
GARSIT
DAIMWY
Oh, sir!!!
IT'S MORE USUAL TO HAVE ONLY HALF OF THIS.

Now arrange the circled letters to form the surprise answer, as suggested by the above cartoon.

Print answer here

1972
PUZZLE
15

JUMBLE®

Unscramble these four Jumbles, one letter to each square, to form four ordinary words.

FECOR

ROBAR

WARMOR

GEPLED

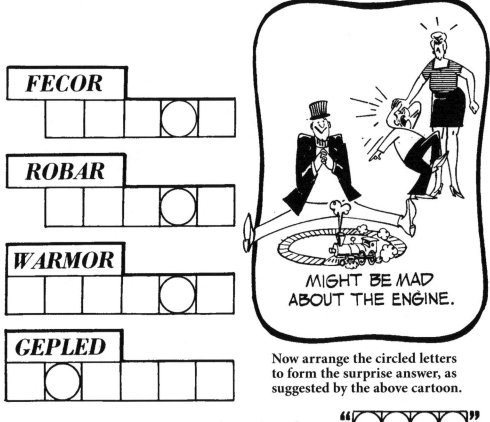

MIGHT BE MAD ABOUT THE ENGINE.

Now arrange the circled letters to form the surprise answer, as suggested by the above cartoon.

Print answer here " "

1972
PUZZLE
16

JUMBLE®

Unscramble these four Jumbles, one letter to each square, to form four ordinary words.

YOIRN

USTEA

SEPPIN

FAINAR

GOES OFF TO REPORT TROUBLE.

Now arrange the circled letters to form the surprise answer, as suggested by the above cartoon.

Print answer here

1972
PUZZLE
17

JUMBLE®

Unscramble these four Jumbles, one letter to each square, to form four ordinary words.

DRUIL

PAWMS

VALERM

HIPLAC

INQUIRIES
COMPLETELY TIED UP IN POSTAL REGULATIONS!

Now arrange the circled letters to form the surprise answer, as suggested by the above cartoon.

Print answer here

1972
PUZZLE
18

JUMBLE®

Unscramble these four Jumbles, one letter to each square, to form four ordinary words.

CILRY
VORAF
TANUBE
DEEMLY
I love 'em all!
HOW THE FAT MAN SPOKE.

Now arrange the circled letters to form the surprise answer, as suggested by the above cartoon.

Print answer here

1972
PUZZLE
19

JUMBLE®

Unscramble these four Jumbles, one letter to each square, to form four ordinary words.

PEINT
AWREY
NURUTE
ERPICH
UNUSUAL TO HAVE A WARM RELATIONSHIP WITH THIS.

Now arrange the circled letters to form the surprise answer, as suggested by the above cartoon.

Print answer here

1972 PUZZLE

20

JUMBLE®

Unscramble these four Jumbles, one letter to each square, to form four ordinary words.

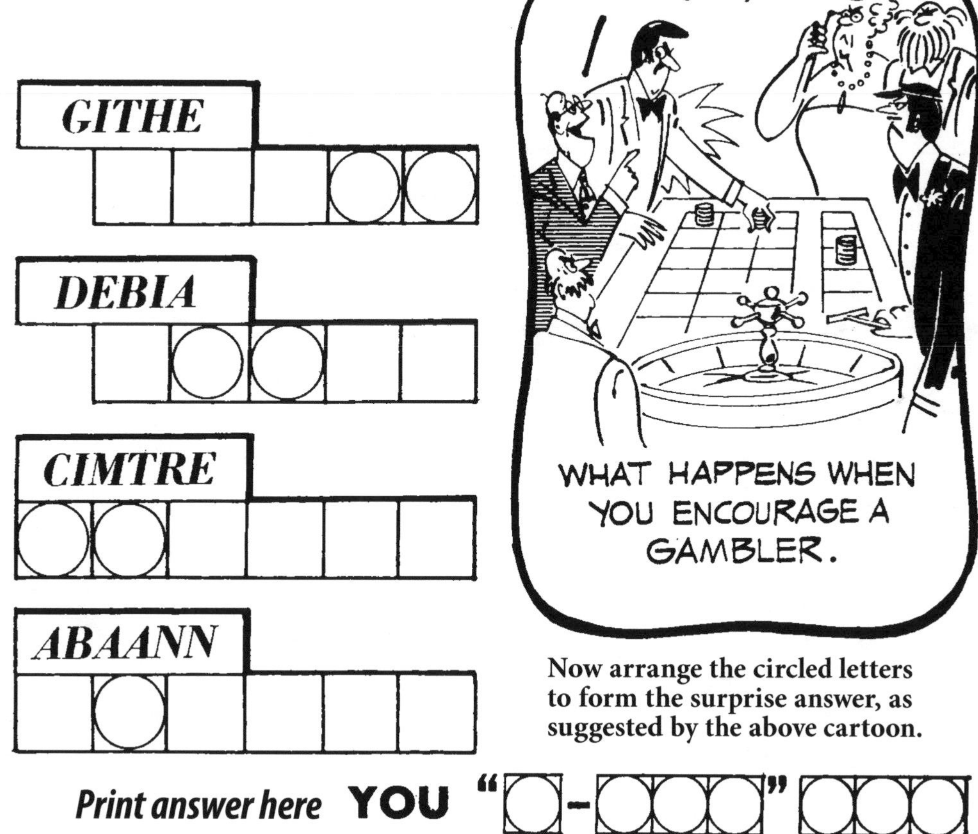

GITHE
DEBIA
CIMTRE
ABAANN
I'm rooting for you
WHAT HAPPENS WHEN YOU ENCOURAGE A GAMBLER.

Now arrange the circled letters to form the surprise answer, as suggested by the above cartoon.

Print answer here **YOU** "◯-◯◯◯◯" ◯◯◯◯

1972
PUZZLE
21

JUMBLE®

Unscramble these four Jumbles, one letter to each square, to form four ordinary words.

COUNE

UFORR

POAFFY

FEECAD

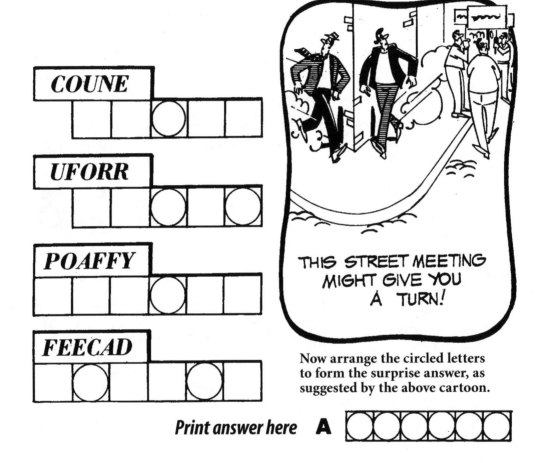

THIS STREET MEETING MIGHT GIVE YOU A TURN!

Now arrange the circled letters to form the surprise answer, as suggested by the above cartoon.

Print answer here **A**

1972 PUZZLE 22

JUMBLE®

Unscramble these four Jumbles, one letter to each square, to form four ordinary words.

YETID

SABSY

LEHBED

PRUSHE

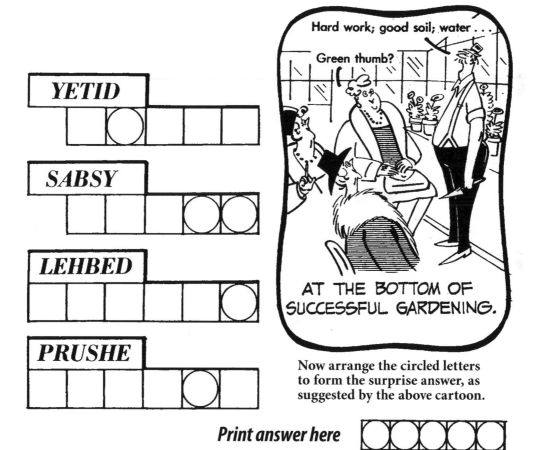

Hard work; good soil; water . . .
Green thumb?
AT THE BOTTOM OF SUCCESSFUL GARDENING.

Now arrange the circled letters to form the surprise answer, as suggested by the above cartoon.

Print answer here 

JUMBLE®

Unscramble these four Jumbles, one letter to each square, to form four ordinary words.

SOMYS

CNATH

EPSOOP

MOYGOL

PALS BROKEN UP IN THE MOUNTAINS.

Now arrange the circled letters to form the surprise answer, as suggested by the above cartoon.

Print answer here

1972
PUZZLE
24

JUMBLE®

Unscramble these four Jumbles, one letter to each square, to form four ordinary words.

INNEL

STAIV

TEPROY

VOXCEN

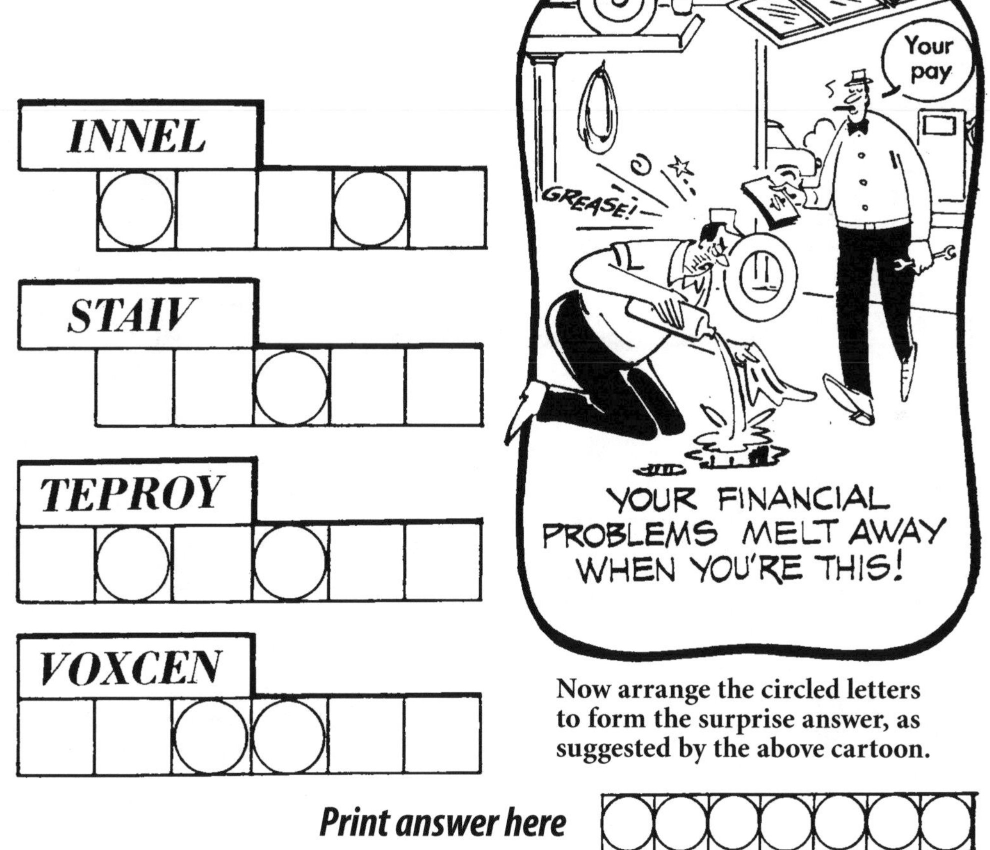
Your pay
GREASE!
YOUR FINANCIAL PROBLEMS MELT AWAY WHEN YOU'RE THIS!

Now arrange the circled letters to form the surprise answer, as suggested by the above cartoon.

Print answer here

1972 PUZZLE 25

JUMBLE®

Unscramble these four Jumbles, one letter to each square, to form four ordinary words.

DAAHE

WOSON

YIRCKT

GELIGG

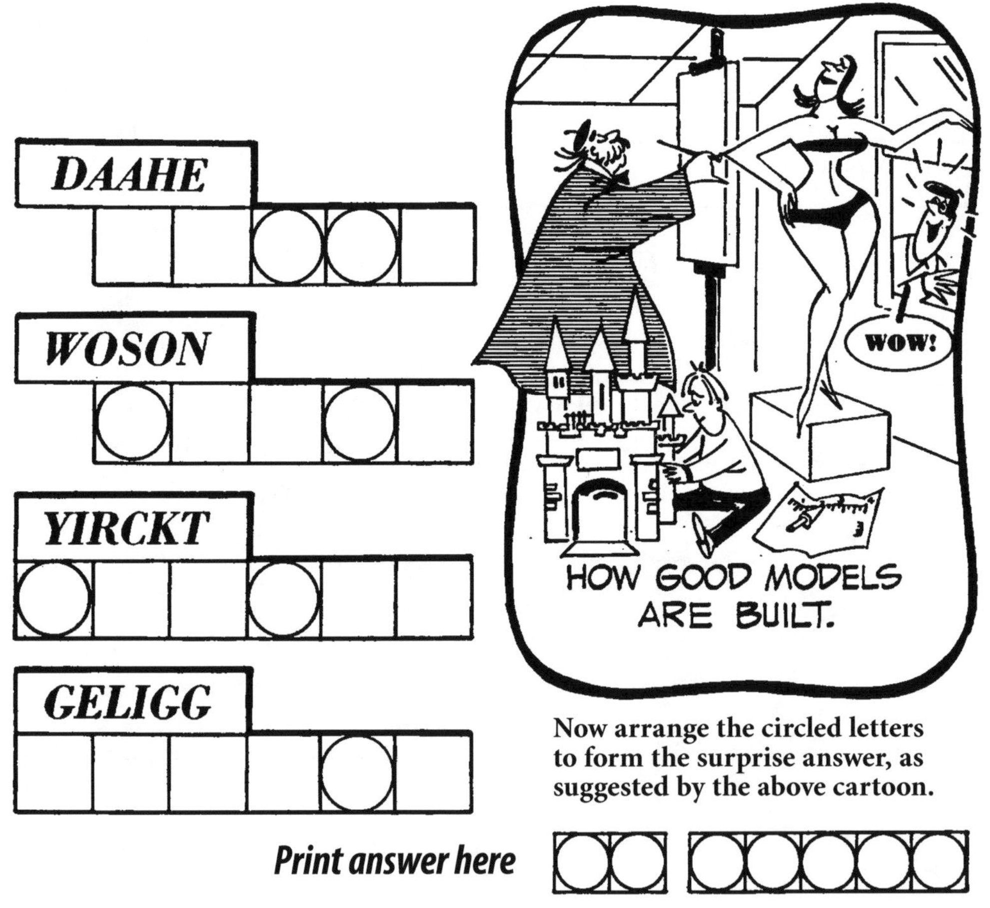
WOW!
HOW GOOD MODELS ARE BUILT.

Now arrange the circled letters to form the surprise answer, as suggested by the above cartoon.

Print answer here

JUMBLE

TIME MACHINE: 1972

Daily Puzzles

1972
PUZZLE
26

JUMBLE®

Unscramble these four Jumbles, one letter to each square, to form four ordinary words.

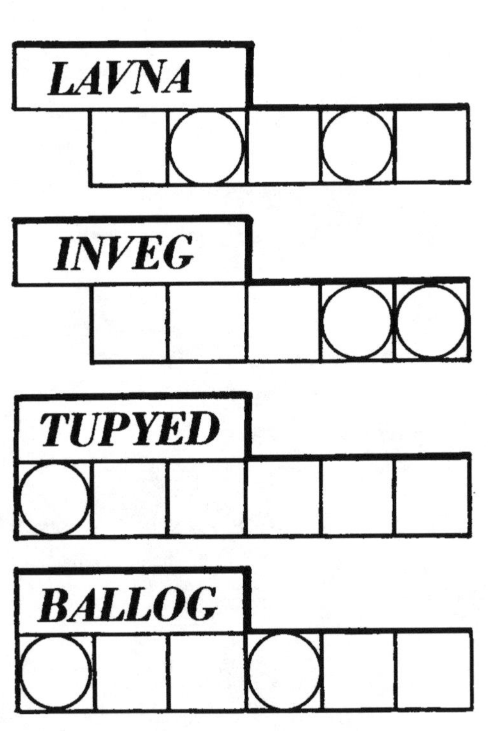
LAVNA
INVEG
TUPYED
BALLOG

SOMETIMES GOES
AROUND TO
PROVIDE COMFORT.

Now arrange the circled letters to form the surprise answer, as suggested by the above cartoon.

Print answer here **A** 

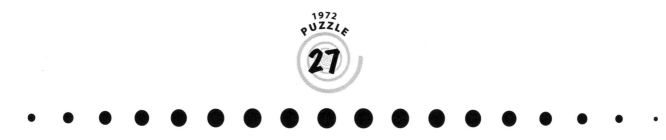

1972
PUZZLE
27

JUMBLE®

Unscramble these four Jumbles, one letter to each square, to form four ordinary words.

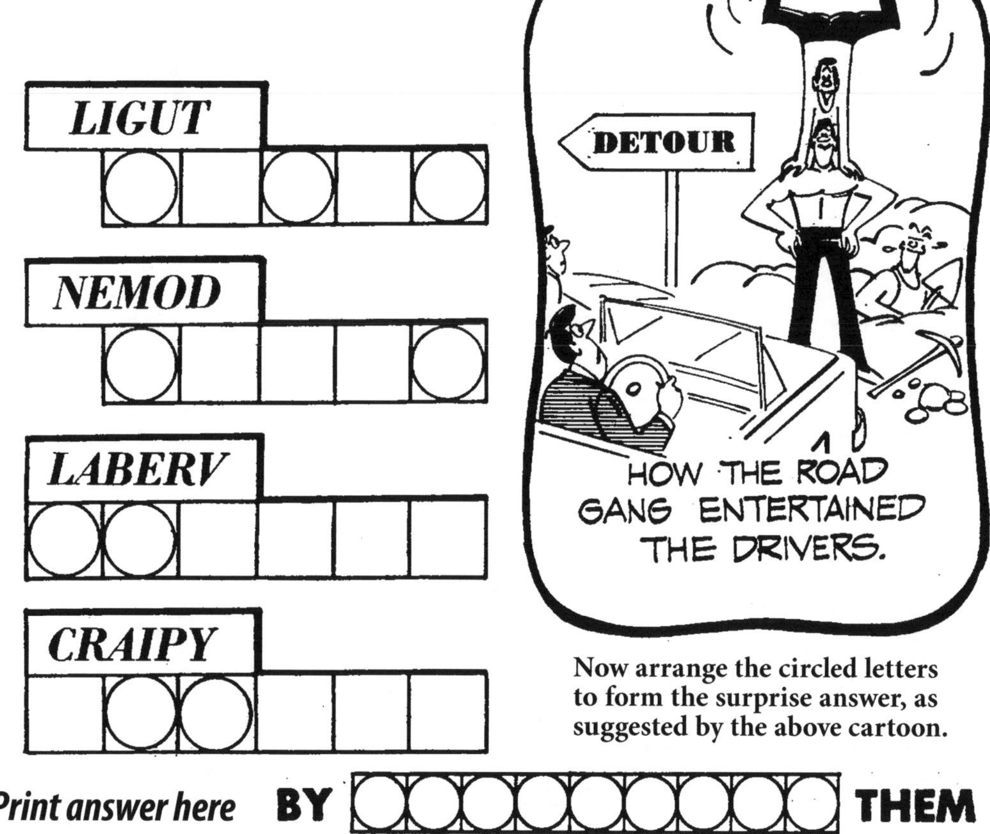
LIGUT
NEMOD
LABERV
CRAIPY
DETOUR
HOW THE ROAD GANG ENTERTAINED THE DRIVERS.

Now arrange the circled letters to form the surprise answer, as suggested by the above cartoon.

Print answer here **BY** ◯◯◯◯◯◯◯◯◯ **THEM**

1972
PUZZLE
28

JUMBLE®

Unscramble these four Jumbles, one letter to each square, to form four ordinary words.

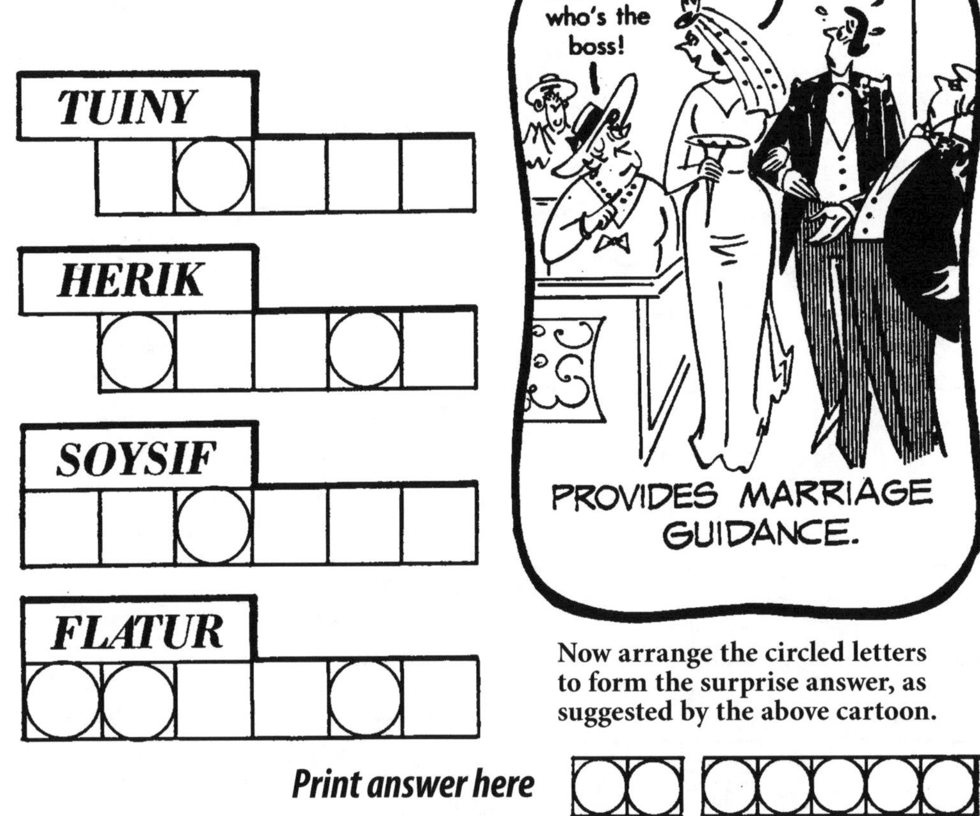
TUINY
HERIK
SOYSIF
FLATUR
Show him who's the boss!
Yes, Mother
PROVIDES MARRIAGE GUIDANCE.

Now arrange the circled letters to form the surprise answer, as suggested by the above cartoon.

Print answer here

1972 PUZZLE 29

JUMBLE®

Unscramble these four Jumbles, one letter to each square, to form four ordinary words.

DRYBE

LIDAP

SHIGLE

CADAFE

JOE'S TATTOO PARLOR
WHAT THE TATTOO ARTIST TURNED GUNMAN DREW ON HIS VICTIMS.

Now arrange the circled letters to form the surprise answer, as suggested by the above cartoon.

Print answer here 

1972
PUZZLE
30

JUMBLE®

Unscramble these four Jumbles, one letter to each square, to form four ordinary words.

GALUH
NYLOP
HILERS
TUNFAL
Thanks for the penny
HOW A MISER PRACTICES PHILANTHROPY.

Now arrange the circled letters to form the surprise answer, as suggested by the above cartoon.

Print answer here

1972
PUZZLE
31

JUMBLE®

Unscramble these four Jumbles, one letter to each square, to form four ordinary words.

VETEN
HORCI
HALTEL
CHECIT
He'll go far
ASS'T.
THIS SHOWS PROMISE.

Now arrange the circled letters to form the surprise answer, as suggested by the above cartoon.

Print answer here **A**

1972
PUZZLE
32

JUMBLE®

Unscramble these four Jumbles, one letter to each square, to form four ordinary words.

KIRPE

TUSEG

SIEMUS

NUHRGY

CAR
RENTAL
AGENCY
THEY CONTRACT TO GIVE YOU A COMFORTABLE RIDE.

Now arrange the circled letters to form the surprise answer, as suggested by the above cartoon.

Print answer here

1972 PUZZLE 33

JUMBLE®

Unscramble these four Jumbles, one letter to each square, to form four ordinary words.

TADAP

NALTS

LUPCOE

YARROS

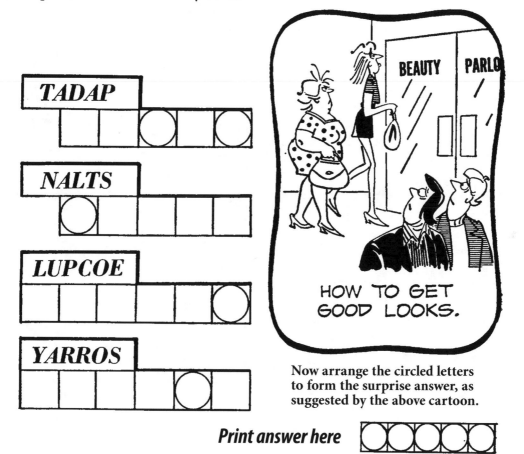

BEAUTY
PARLO
HOW TO GET GOOD LOOKS.

Now arrange the circled letters to form the surprise answer, as suggested by the above cartoon.

Print answer here

1972
PUZZLE
34

JUMBLE®

Unscramble these four Jumbles, one letter to each square, to form four ordinary words.

ATAGE

EFING

YONDOB

MOCNOM

No telephone calls . . .
No loud records . . .
She's new
APERS
HE WON'T STAND FOR ANYTHING!

Now arrange the circled letters to form the surprise answer, as suggested by the above cartoon.

Print answer here

1972 PUZZLE

35

JUMBLE®

Unscramble these four Jumbles, one letter to each square, to form four ordinary words.

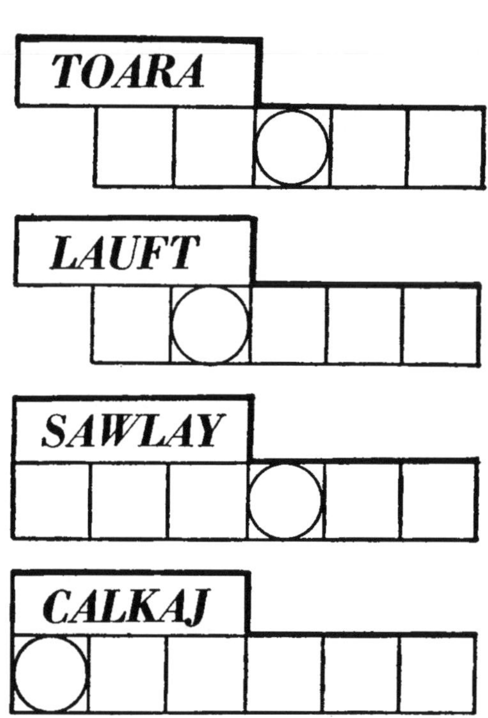

TOARA
LAUFT
SAWLAY
CALKAJ

BEWARE OF DOG
HOW NOT TO LEAVE A DOOR IF YOU DON'T WANT THEM TO STEAL A VASE.

Now arrange the circled letters to form the surprise answer, as suggested by the above cartoon.

Print answer here 

1972
PUZZLE
36

JUMBLE®

Unscramble these four Jumbles, one letter to each square, to form four ordinary words.

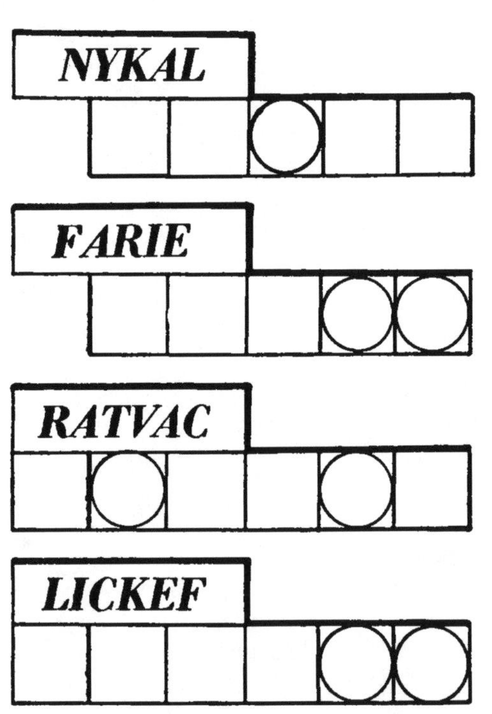
NYKAL
FARIE
RATVAC
LICKEF

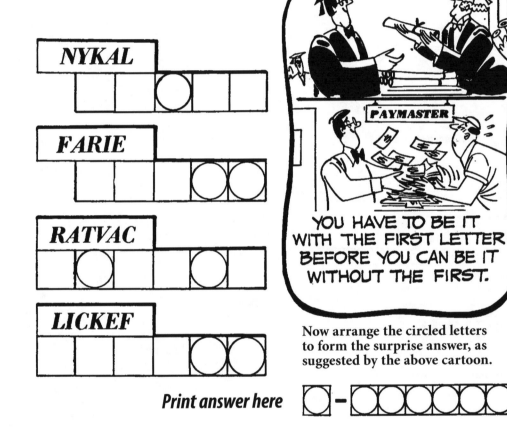

PAYMASTER
YOU HAVE TO BE IT WITH THE FIRST LETTER BEFORE YOU CAN BE IT WITHOUT THE FIRST.

Now arrange the circled letters to form the surprise answer, as suggested by the above cartoon.

Print answer here ◯-◯◯◯◯◯◯

1972 PUZZLE

37

JUMBLE®

Unscramble these four Jumbles, one letter to each square, to form four ordinary words.

TIELE
SLARN
POATIE
ROTRAM
Is this the place for the opening?
GALLERY
THEATER PERFORMANCES NOT OPEN TO THE PUBLIC.

Now arrange the circled letters to form the surprise answer, as suggested by the above cartoon.

Print answer here

1972
PUZZLE
38

JUMBLE®

Unscramble these four Jumbles, one letter to each square, to form four ordinary words.

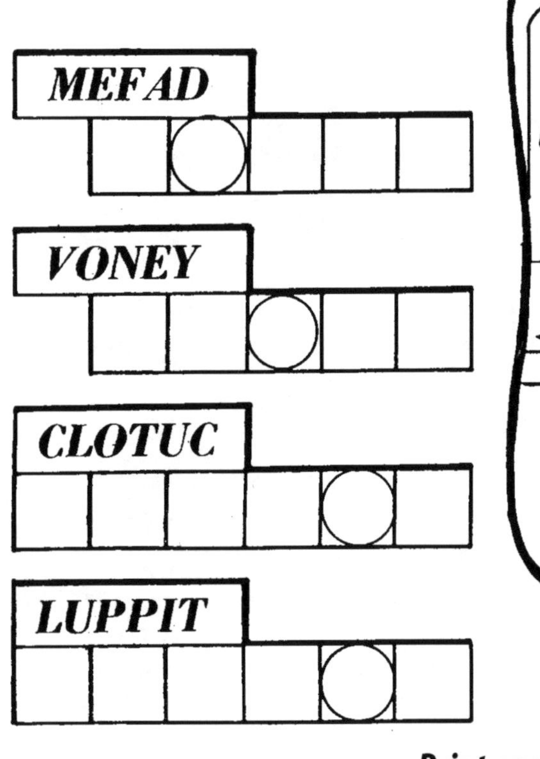
MEFAD
VONEY
CLOTUC
LUPPIT

Who's next, Lucrezia?
Him!
SOMETIMES CARRIES POISON AND SOUNDS AWFUL.

Now arrange the circled letters to form the surprise answer, as suggested by the above cartoon.

Print answer here 

1972 PUZZLE

39

JUMBLE®

Unscramble these four Jumbles, one letter to each square, to form four ordinary words.

USOED

GINOR

FLOAFY

RAYPER

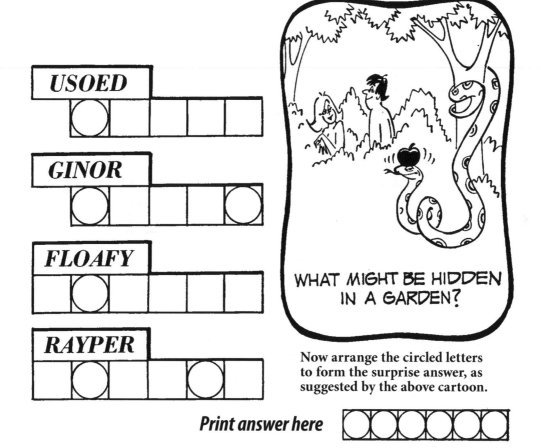

WHAT MIGHT BE HIDDEN IN A GARDEN?

Now arrange the circled letters to form the surprise answer, as suggested by the above cartoon.

Print answer here

1972
PUZZLE
40

JUMBLE®

Unscramble these four Jumbles, one letter to each square, to form four ordinary words.

IPPUL

LOVEH

SCUSID

RAZTUQ

He charges too much
$
THIS WOULD DESCRIBE A HIGH-SPIRITED CHISELER.

Now arrange the circled letters to form the surprise answer, as suggested by the above cartoon.

Print answer here "○○○○○○○"

1972
PUZZLE
41

JUMBLE®

Unscramble these four Jumbles, one letter to each square, to form four ordinary words.

YIRDT

GANGI

CADILP

INLOIV

His total alibi blah blah . . .
THIS IS USED IN SUMMING UP.

Now arrange the circled letters to form the surprise answer, as suggested by the above cartoon.

Print answer here

1972
PUZZLE
42

JUMBLE®

Unscramble these four Jumbles, one letter to each square, to form four ordinary words.

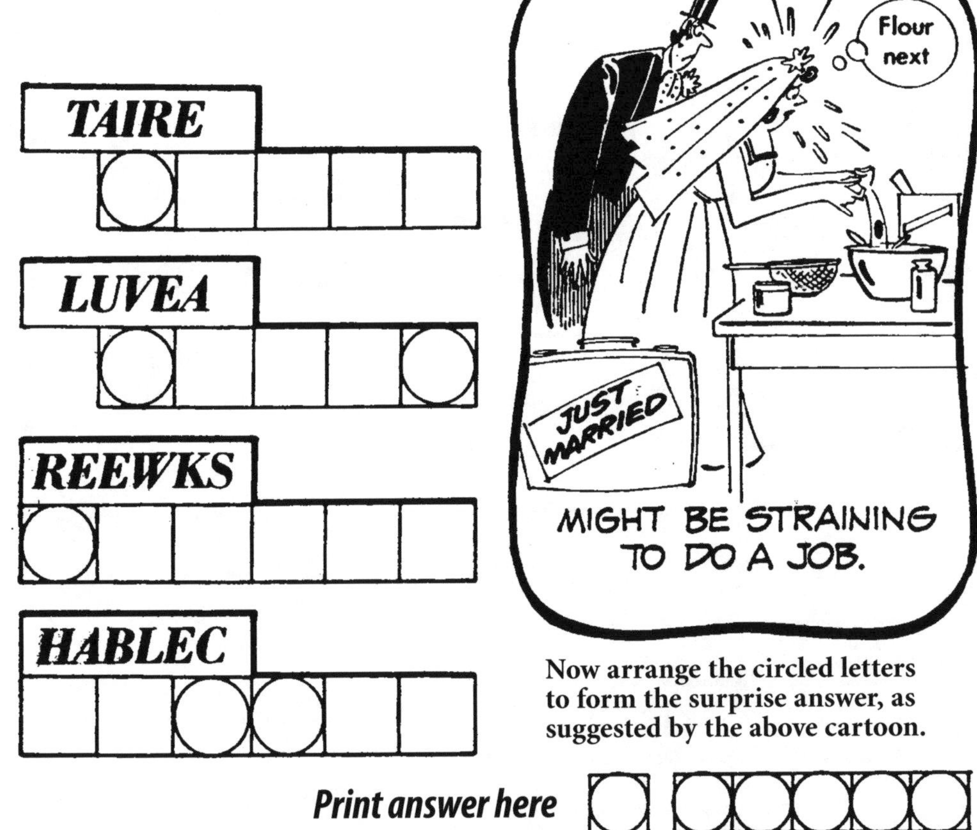
TAIRE
LUVEA
REEWKS
HABLEC
Flour next
JUST MARRIED
MIGHT BE STRAINING TO DO A JOB.

Now arrange the circled letters to form the surprise answer, as suggested by the above cartoon.

Print answer here

1972
PUZZLE
43

JUMBLE®

Unscramble these four Jumbles, one letter to each square, to form four ordinary words.

LIVIG

KNAWE

HERTHS

WEARLY

WANT ADS
THIS VIEW MAY HELP YOU GET A JOB.

Now arrange the circled letters to form the surprise answer, as suggested by the above cartoon.

Print answer here **AN**

1972
PUZZLE
44

JUMBLE®

Unscramble these four Jumbles, one letter to each square, to form four ordinary words.

YASID

RECEL

OURSEA

DRUTSY

Here are your notes
THEY INSURE THE CORRECT DELIVERY OF SPEECHES.

Now arrange the circled letters to form the surprise answer, as suggested by the above cartoon.

Print answer here

1972
PUZZLE
45

JUMBLE®

Unscramble these four Jumbles, one letter to each square, to form four ordinary words.

KEWOA

INORM

TINCLE

TOBENN

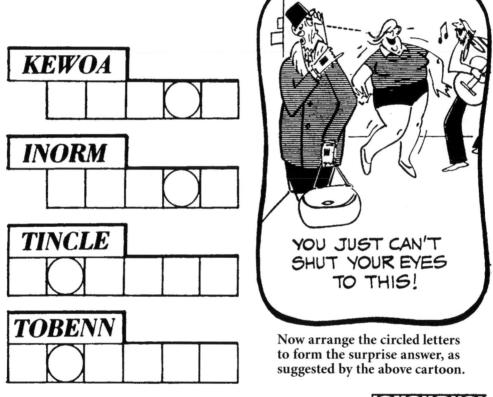

YOU JUST CAN'T SHUT YOUR EYES TO THIS!

Now arrange the circled letters to form the surprise answer, as suggested by the above cartoon.

Print answer here 

1972
PUZZLE
46

JUMBLE®

Unscramble these four Jumbles, one letter to each square, to form four ordinary words.

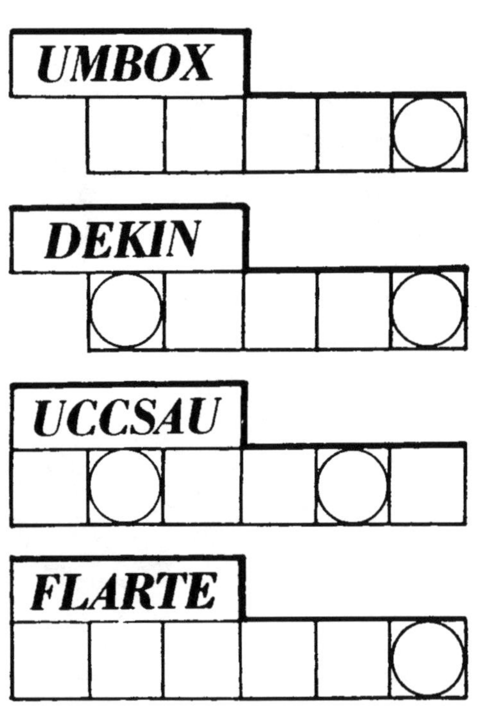
UMBOX
DEKIN
UCCSAU
FLARTE

You can see it in the dark
THIS MIGHT BE COMPOSED OF MUD AND AIR.

Now arrange the circled letters to form the surprise answer, as suggested by the above cartoon.

Print answer here

1972
PUZZLE
47

JUMBLE®

Unscramble these four Jumbles, one letter to each square, to form four ordinary words.

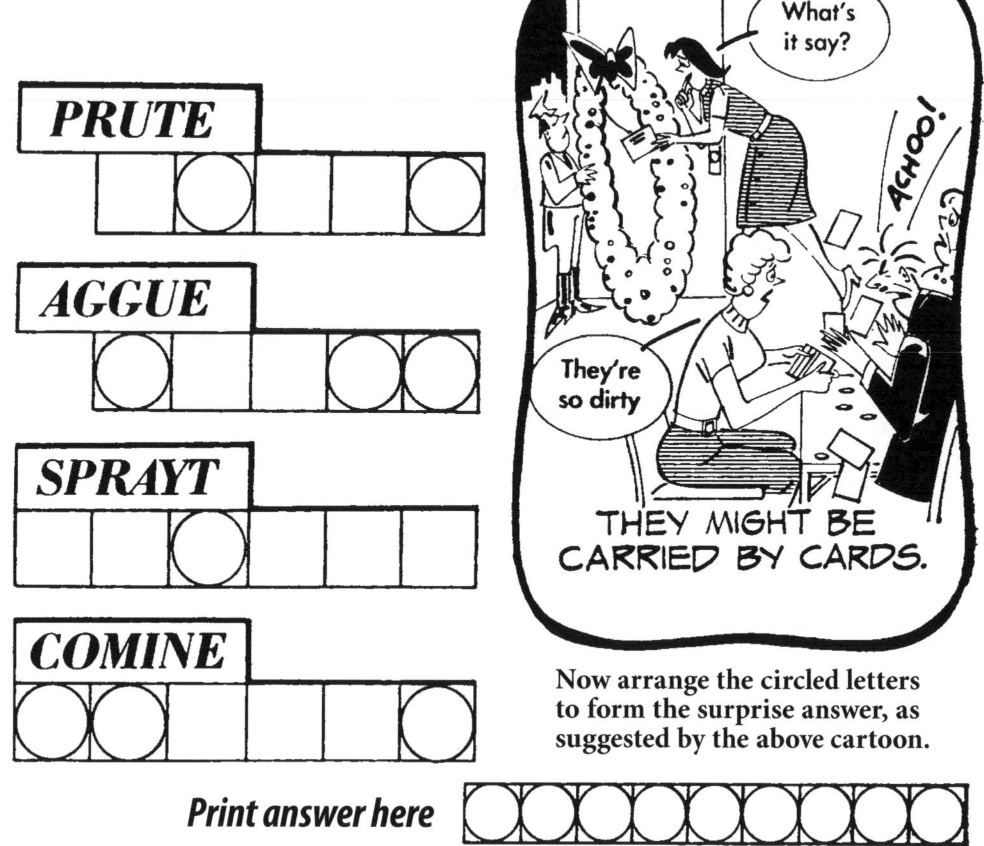
PRUTE
AGGUE
SPRAYT
COMINE
What's it say?
ACHOO!
They're so dirty
THEY MIGHT BE CARRIED BY CARDS.

Now arrange the circled letters to form the surprise answer, as suggested by the above cartoon.

Print answer here

1972
PUZZLE
48

JUMBLE®

Unscramble these four Jumbles, one letter to each square, to form four ordinary words.

GUBEN

ORVAS

SHRAIG

TORFIP

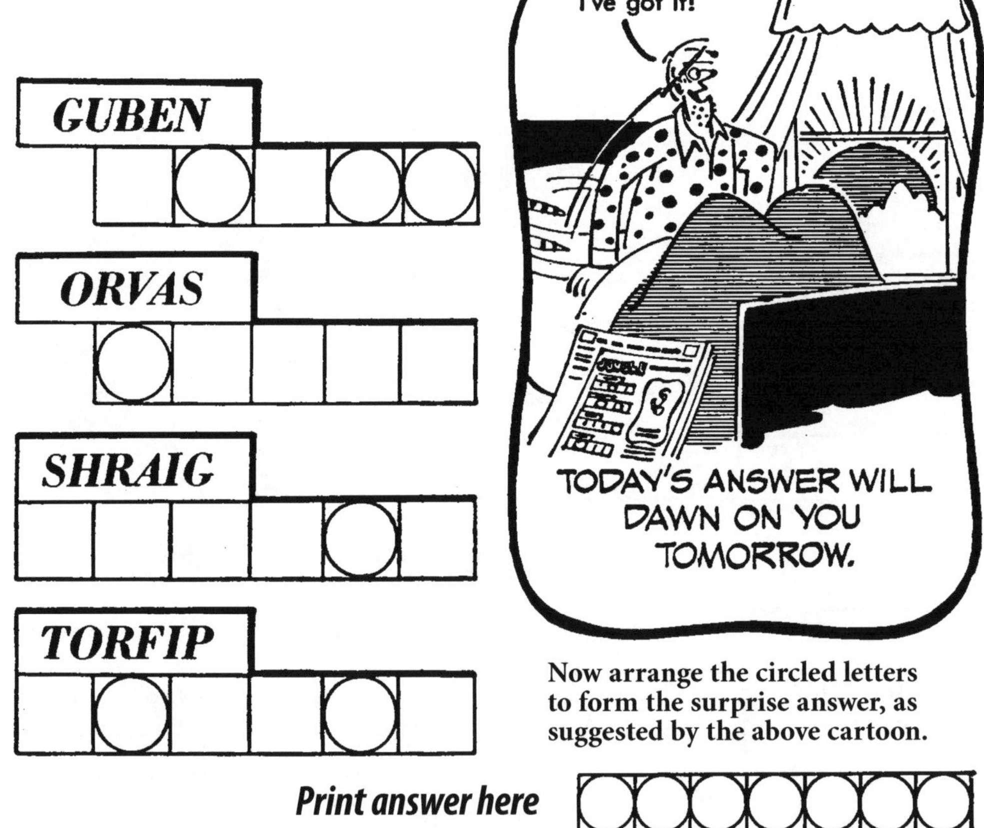
I've got it!
TODAY'S ANSWER WILL DAWN ON YOU TOMORROW.

Now arrange the circled letters to form the surprise answer, as suggested by the above cartoon.

Print answer here

1972
PUZZLE
49

JUMBLE®

Unscramble these four Jumbles, one letter to each square, to form four ordinary words.

BROEP
DRATY
LADLAB
BONGIB
TOBACCONI
P.D.
WHAT HE WAS WAS APPARENT.

Now arrange the circled letters to form the surprise answer, as suggested by the above cartoon.

Print answer here

1972
PUZZLE
50

JUMBLE®

Unscramble these four Jumbles, one letter to each square, to form four ordinary words.

MUPIO
NOJEY
TRALEY
DRIZAL
Huh?
ONCE AROUSED YOU MAY LOSE IT!

Now arrange the circled letters to form the surprise answer, as suggested by the above cartoon.

Print answer here

JUMBLE®

Unscramble these four Jumbles, one letter to each square, to form four ordinary words.

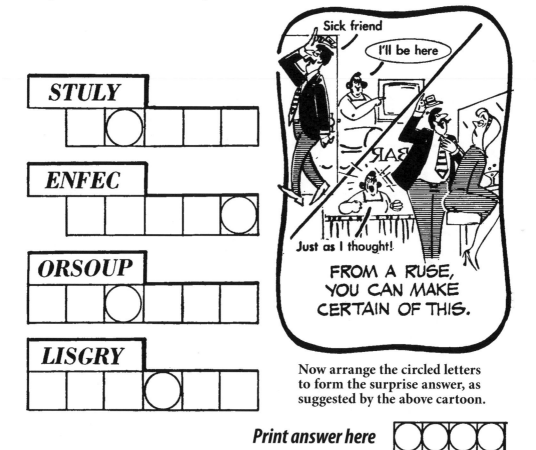

STULY
ENFEC
ORSOUP
LISGRY
Sick friend
I'll be here
BAR
Just as I thought!
FROM A RUSE, YOU CAN MAKE CERTAIN OF THIS.

Now arrange the circled letters to form the surprise answer, as suggested by the above cartoon.

Print answer here

1972
PUZZLE
52

JUMBLE®

Unscramble these four Jumbles, one letter to each square, to form four ordinary words.

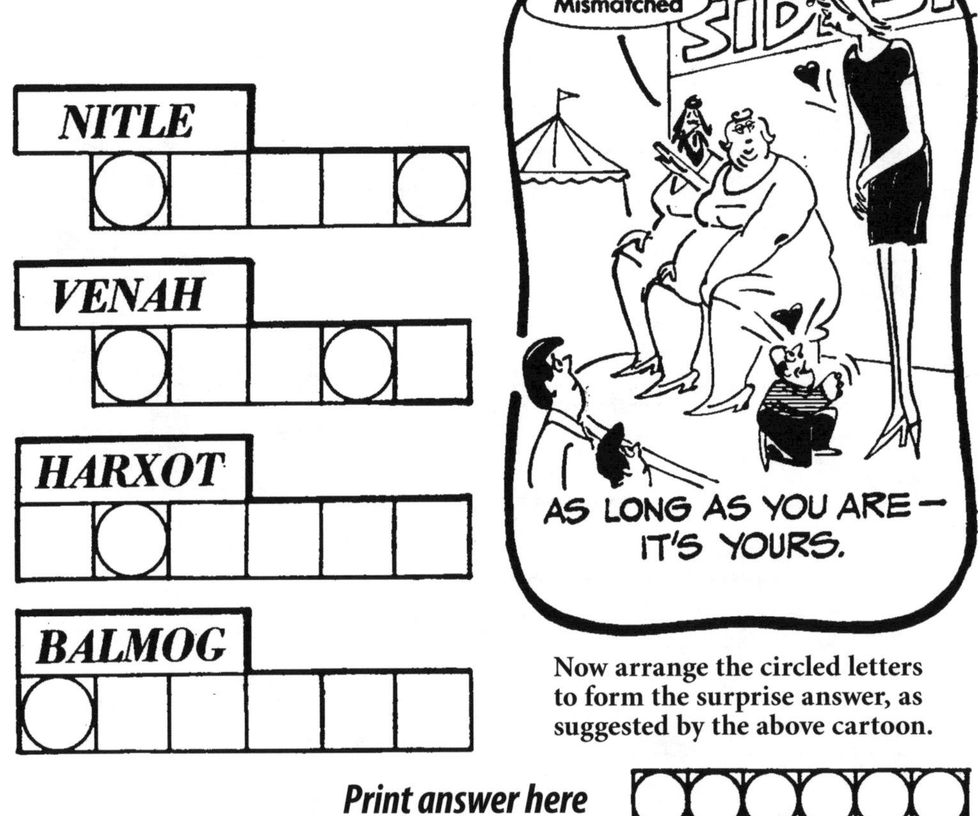
NITLE
VENAH
HARXOT
BALMOG
Mismatched
SID
AS LONG AS YOU ARE — IT'S YOURS.

Now arrange the circled letters to form the surprise answer, as suggested by the above cartoon.

Print answer here

1972 PUZZLE

53

JUMBLE®

Unscramble these four Jumbles, one letter to each square, to form four ordinary words.

TEAHB

YEEPA

DOULCY

EXCOIB

RAN DOWN THE BEACH.

Now arrange the circled letters to form the surprise answer, as suggested by the above cartoon.

Print answer here

1972
PUZZLE
54

JUMBLE®

Unscramble these four Jumbles, one letter to each square, to form four ordinary words.

COPHE

PRAAT

BATEEK

ORFALL

Fire the man responsible for this!
NEW DISCLOSURES
MIGHT MEAN SOME DRIP LET THE SECRETS OUT.

Now arrange the circled letters to form the surprise answer, as suggested by the above cartoon.

Print answer here ☐ "☐☐☐☐"

1972 PUZZLE

55

JUMBLE®

Unscramble these four Jumbles, one letter to each square, to form four ordinary words.

EVVER
OTTOH
CEIVED
RABENN
Jury is back
TRY AND GIVE THIS TO A PRISONER.

Now arrange the circled letters to form the surprise answer, as suggested by the above cartoon.

Print answer here

JUMBLE®

Unscramble these four Jumbles, one letter to each square, to form four ordinary words.

USVEA

DYNAH

WERDOP

QUILID

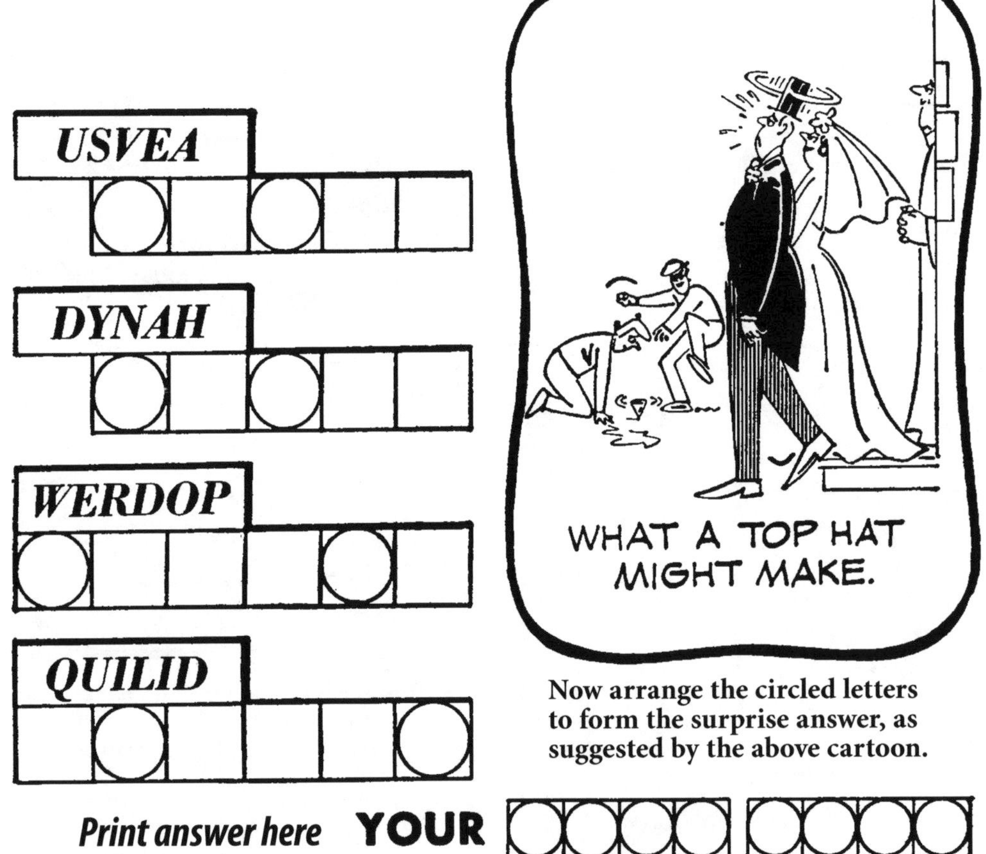
WHAT A TOP HAT MIGHT MAKE.

Now arrange the circled letters to form the surprise answer, as suggested by the above cartoon.

Print answer here YOUR

1972
PUZZLE
57

JUMBLE®

Unscramble these four Jumbles, one letter to each square, to form four ordinary words.

SUMIC

PETIR

NAWDDE

ENIAMA

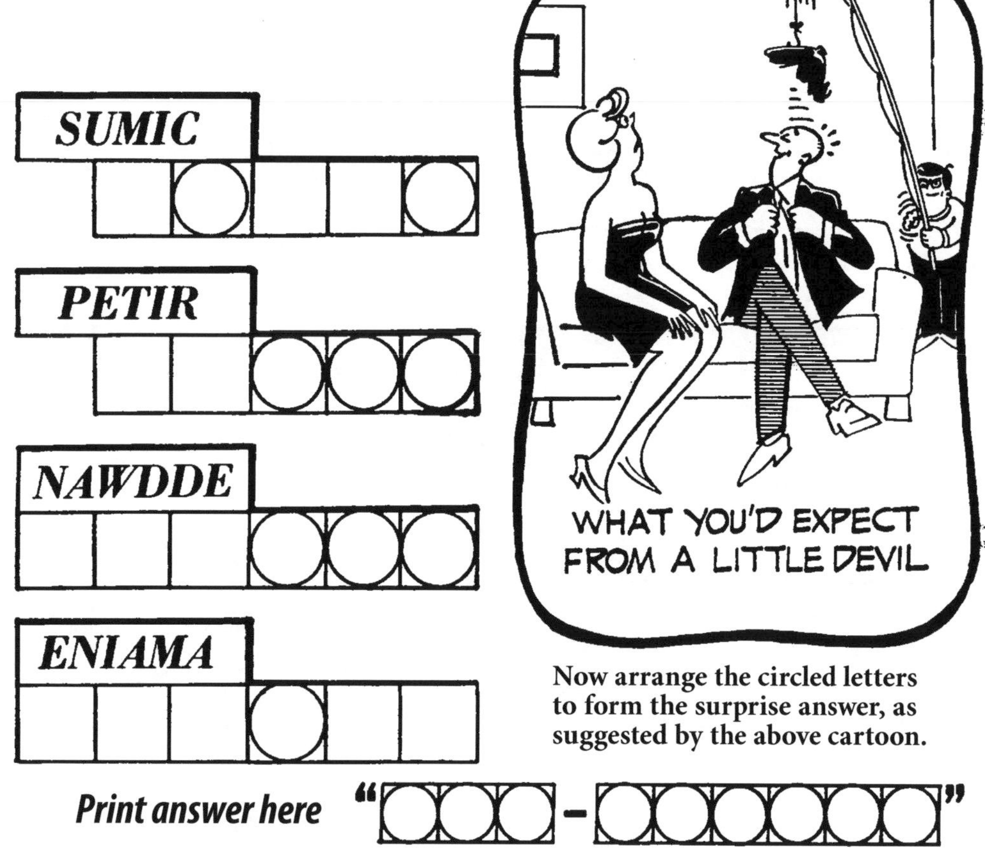
WHAT YOU'D EXPECT FROM A LITTLE DEVIL

Now arrange the circled letters to form the surprise answer, as suggested by the above cartoon.

Print answer here "___-______"

1972
PUZZLE
58

JUMBLE®

Unscramble these four Jumbles, one letter to each square, to form four ordinary words.

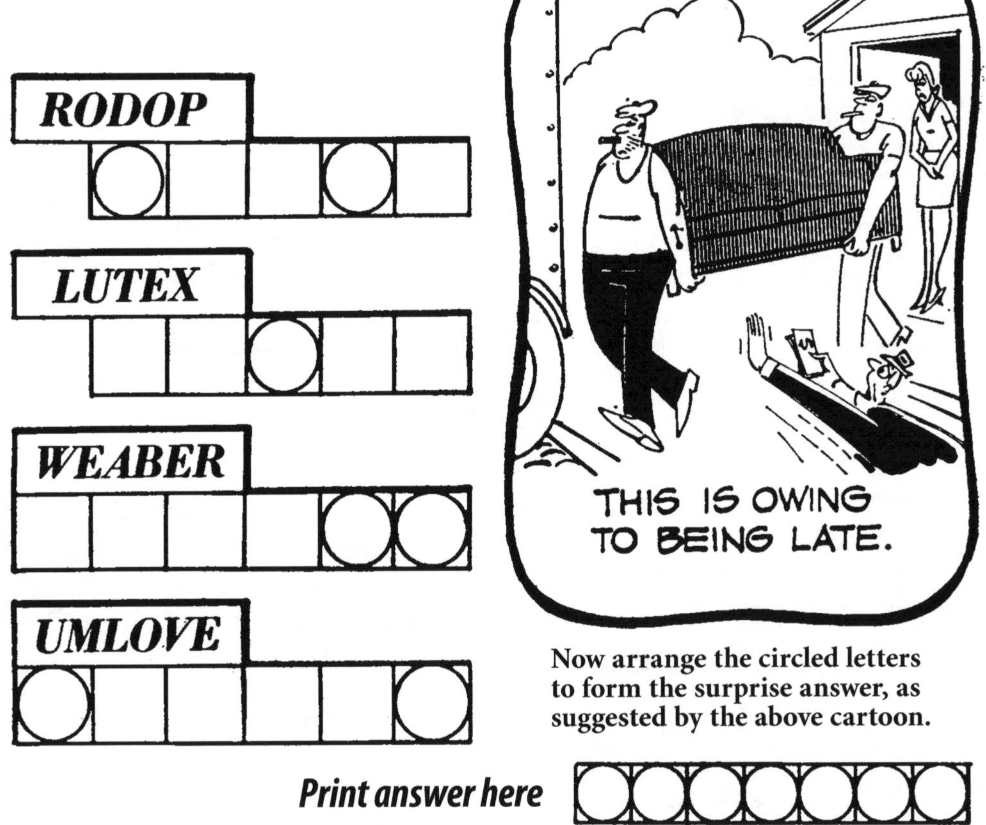
RODOP
LUTEX
WEABER
UMLOVE
THIS IS OWING
TO BEING LATE.

Now arrange the circled letters to form the surprise answer, as suggested by the above cartoon.

Print answer here

1972 PUZZLE

59

JUMBLE®

Unscramble these four Jumbles, one letter to each square, to form four ordinary words.

WENYL

NABOR

LENPOL

UNTAUM

COUNSELOR
Happens all the time
MAKE NOTHING OF IT!

Now arrange the circled letters to form the surprise answer, as suggested by the above cartoon.

Print answer here 

1972
PUZZLE
60

JUMBLE®

Unscramble these four Jumbles, one letter to each square, to form four ordinary words.

VUMEA

CITHY

RUFUTE

RYMILG

THEY DO LIKE EACH OTHER.

Now arrange the circled letters to form the surprise answer, as suggested by the above cartoon.

Print answer here

1972
PUZZLE
61

JUMBLE®

Unscramble these four Jumbles, one letter to each square, to form four ordinary words.

DRAIC

TRAFD

MIRAPI

ZYNEEM

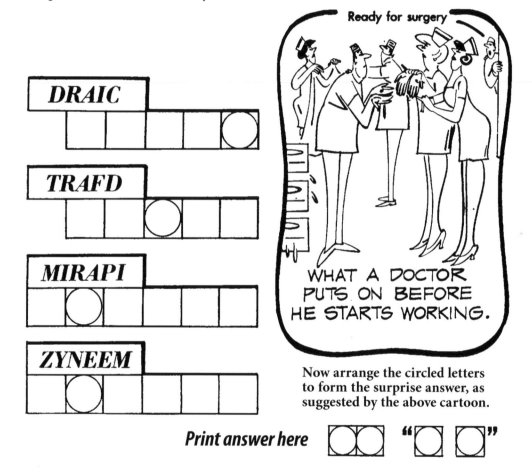

Ready for surgery

WHAT A DOCTOR PUTS ON BEFORE HE STARTS WORKING.

Now arrange the circled letters to form the surprise answer, as suggested by the above cartoon.

Print answer here

1972
PUZZLE
62

JUMBLE®

Unscramble these four Jumbles, one letter to each square, to form four ordinary words.

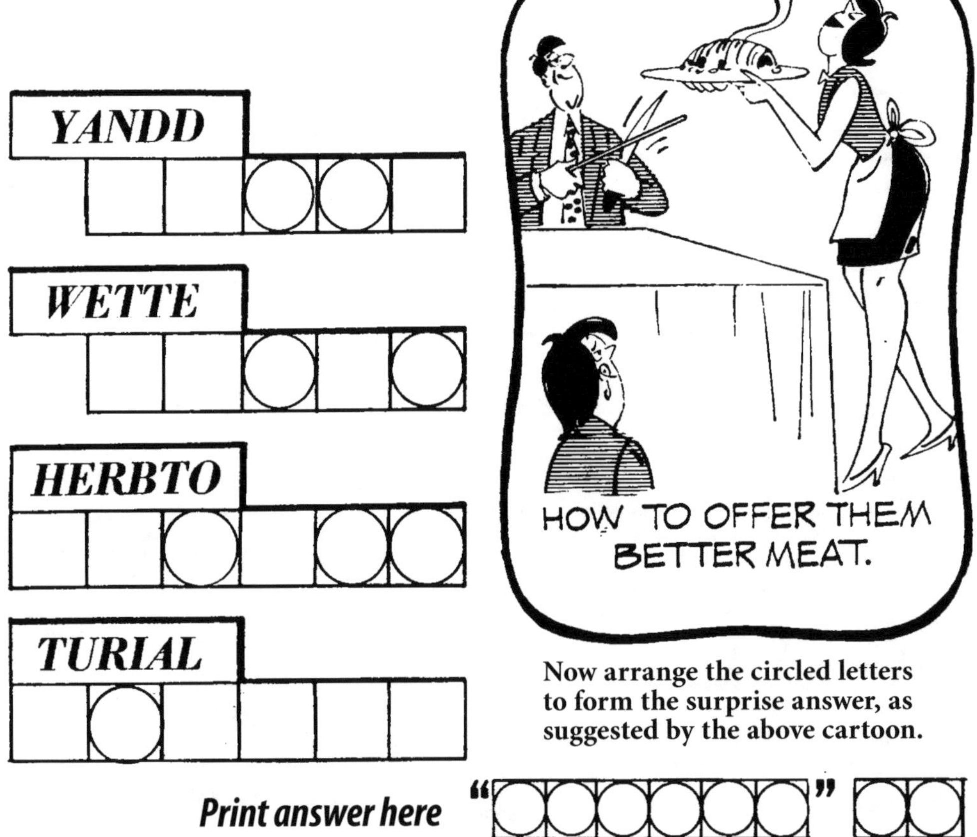
YANDD
WETTE
HERBTO
TURIAL
HOW TO OFFER THEM BETTER MEAT.

Now arrange the circled letters to form the surprise answer, as suggested by the above cartoon.

Print answer here “ ◯◯◯◯◯◯ ” ◯◯

1972
PUZZLE
63

JUMBLE®

Unscramble these four Jumbles, one letter to each square, to form four ordinary words.

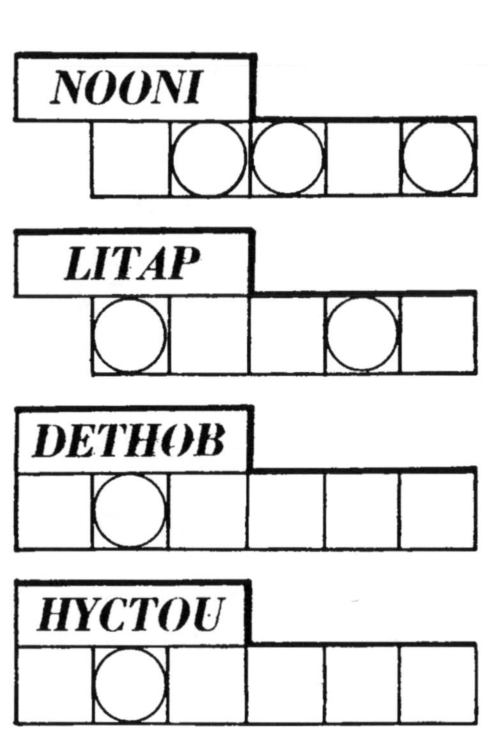
NOONI
LITAP
DETHOB
HYCTOU

Gimme that!
POLITICAL DEBATE
WHAT YOU THINK IS YOURS.

Now arrange the circled letters to form the surprise answer, as suggested by the above cartoon.

Print answer here

1972
PUZZLE
64

JUMBLE®

Unscramble these four Jumbles, one letter to each square, to form four ordinary words.

LOOGI

RAVOL

TALMEL

GINCHA

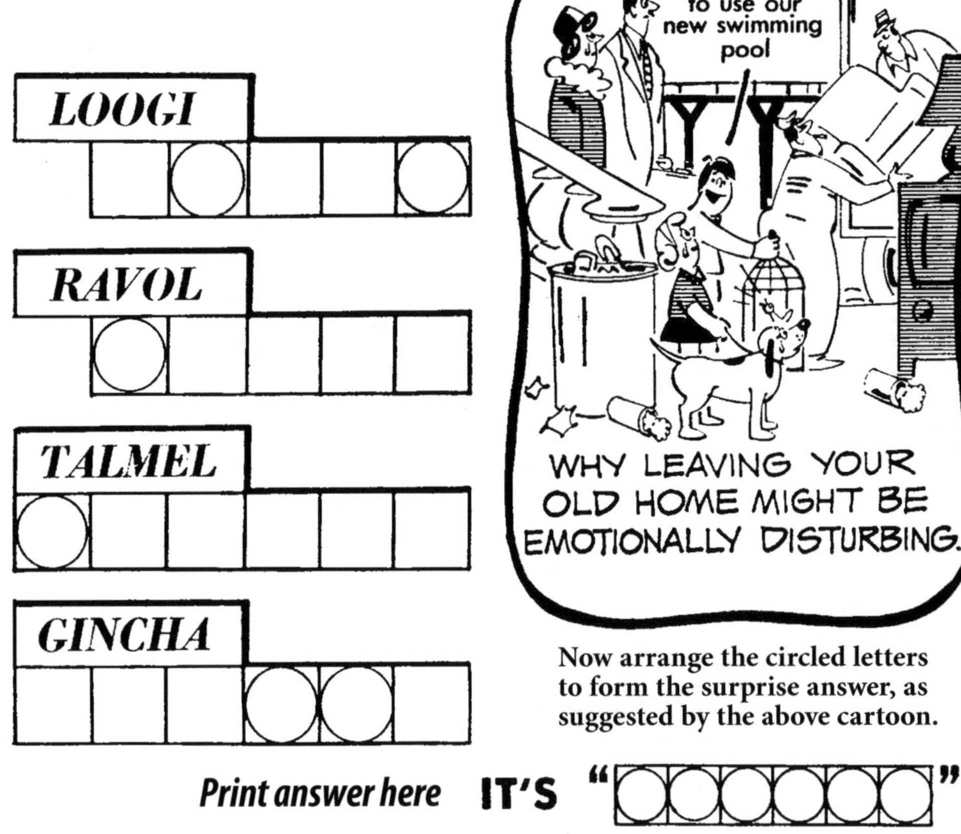
Can't wait to use our new swimming pool
WHY LEAVING YOUR OLD HOME MIGHT BE EMOTIONALLY DISTURBING.

Now arrange the circled letters to form the surprise answer, as suggested by the above cartoon.

Print answer here **IT'S** "   "

1972
PUZZLE
65

JUMBLE®

Unscramble these four Jumbles, one letter to each square, to form four ordinary words.

GOUNY

CANYF

NEPPAH

YIVELT

Regarding that shipment of underwear—

Oops! My wife!

MAKES MANY A SLIP!

Now arrange the circled letters to form the surprise answer, as suggested by the above cartoon.

Print answer here

1972
PUZZLE
66

JUMBLE®

Unscramble these four Jumbles, one letter to each square, to form four ordinary words.

CHALT
LEEBI
KENASH
ROMMIE

SALE
FOR
MILLIONAIRES
ONLY
MIGHT BE IN THE SALE AT THE FUR SHOP.

Now arrange the circled letters to form the surprise answer, as suggested by the above cartoon.

Print answer here

1972
PUZZLE
67

JUMBLE®

Unscramble these four Jumbles, one letter to each square, to form four ordinary words.

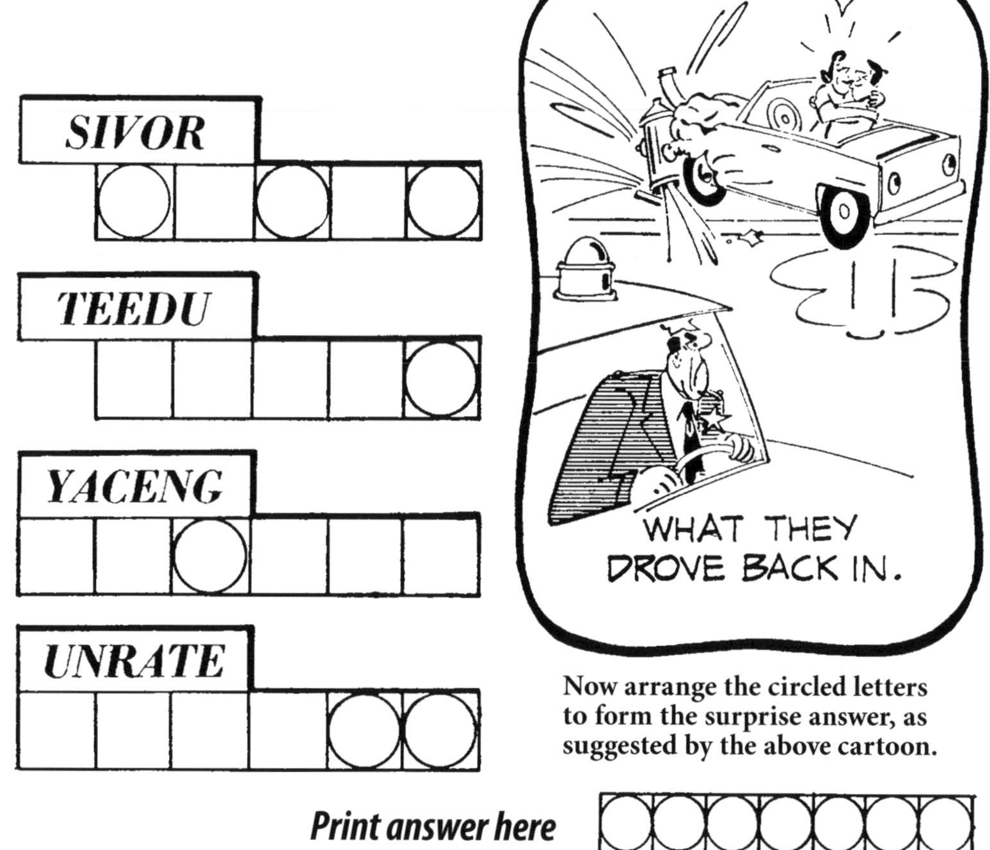
SIVOR
TEEDU
YACENG
UNRATE
WHAT THEY DROVE BACK IN.

Now arrange the circled letters to form the surprise answer, as suggested by the above cartoon.

Print answer here

1972
PUZZLE
68

JUMBLE®

Unscramble these four Jumbles, one letter to each square, to form four ordinary words.

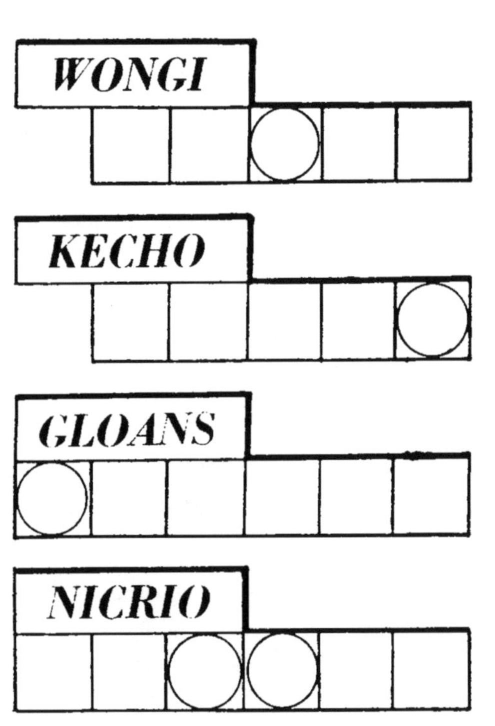
WONGI
KECHO
GLOANS
NICRIO

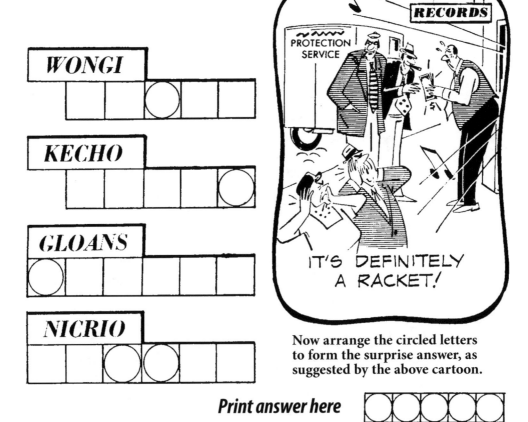

RECORDS
PROTECTION
SERVICE
IT'S DEFINITELY A RACKET!

Now arrange the circled letters to form the surprise answer, as suggested by the above cartoon.

Print answer here

1972 PUZZLE

69

JUMBLE®

Unscramble these four Jumbles, one letter to each square, to form four ordinary words.

LESOO

SILAA

TORMAN

PLOGES

Some celebration!

FESTIVITY WITH A GAL.

Now arrange the circled letters to form the surprise answer, as suggested by the above cartoon.

Print answer here 

1972
PUZZLE
70

JUMBLE®

Unscramble these four Jumbles, one letter to each square, to form four ordinary words.

TABEA

HARNC

INKIIB

UNPRIT

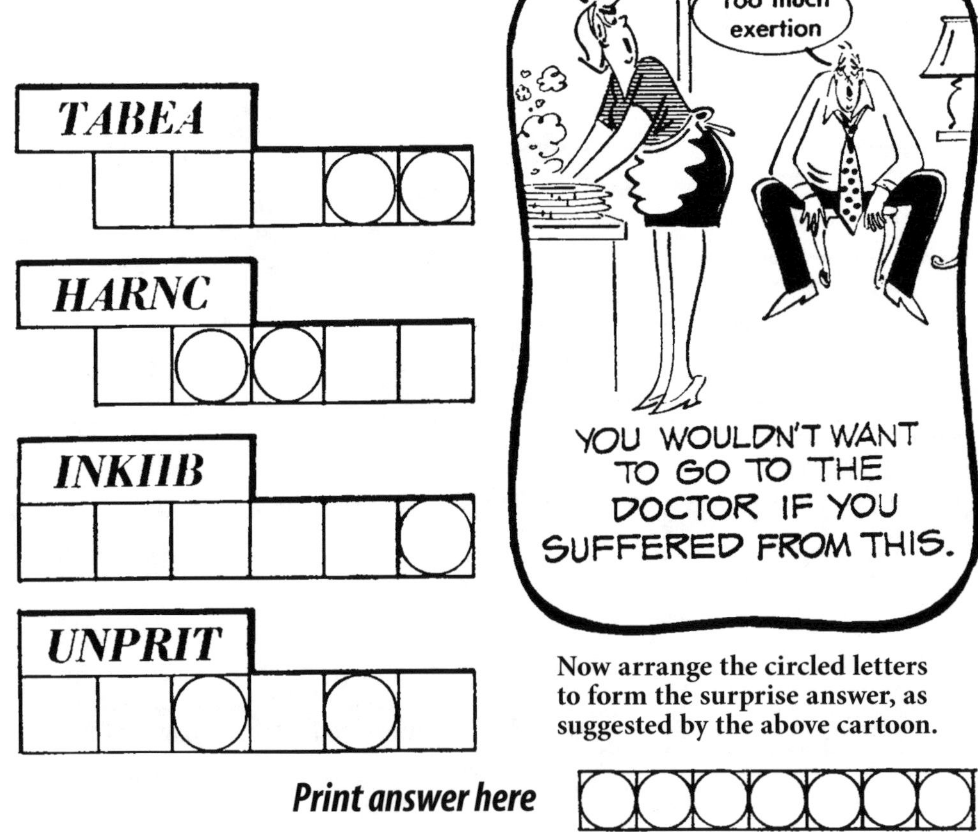

Go see him
Too much exertion
YOU WOULDN'T WANT TO GO TO THE DOCTOR IF YOU SUFFERED FROM THIS.

Now arrange the circled letters to form the surprise answer, as suggested by the above cartoon.

Print answer here

1972
PUZZLE
71

JUMBLE®

Unscramble these four Jumbles, one letter to each square, to form four ordinary words.

RINDE

VORLE

BOADUN

DARNBY

RAT TAT TAT

JUMBLE

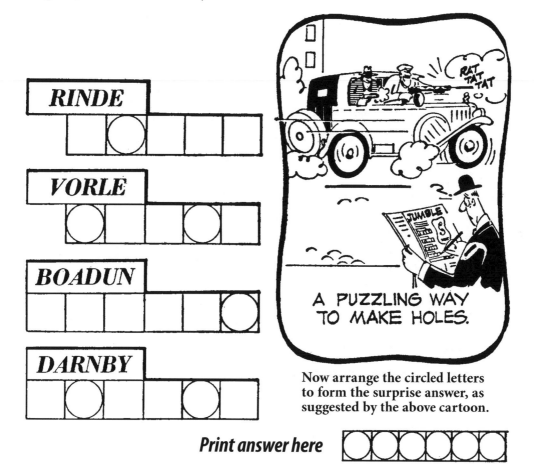

A PUZZLING WAY TO MAKE HOLES.

Now arrange the circled letters to form the surprise answer, as suggested by the above cartoon.

Print answer here

1972
PUZZLE
72

JUMBLE®

Unscramble these four Jumbles, one letter to each square, to form four ordinary words.

VENOL

PIGER

BROSAB

DAYNIT

PROVIDES THE MAIN COURSE ON BOARD SHIP.

Now arrange the circled letters to form the surprise answer, as suggested by the above cartoon.

Print answer here **THE**

1972
PUZZLE
73

JUMBLE®

Unscramble these four Jumbles, one letter to each square, to form four ordinary words.

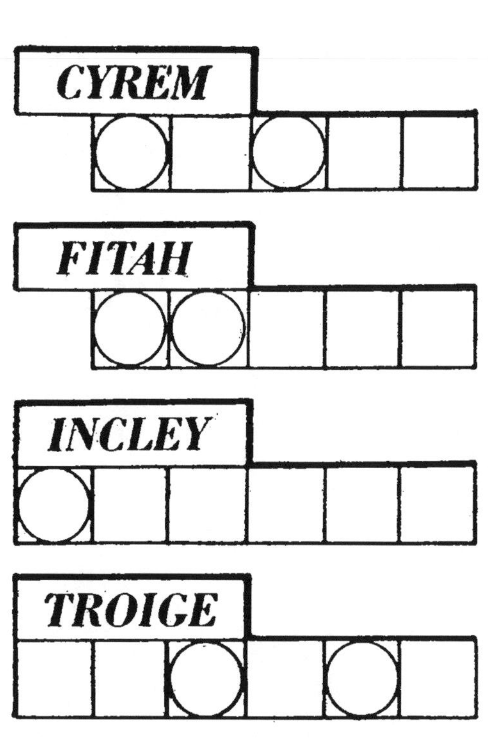

CYREM
FITAH
INCLEY
TROIGE

Hurry!

TELL THIS GUY TO GO TO BLAZES—AND YOU'LL GET A RESPONSE OUT OF HIM!

Now arrange the circled letters to form the surprise answer, as suggested by the above cartoon.

Print answer here **A** 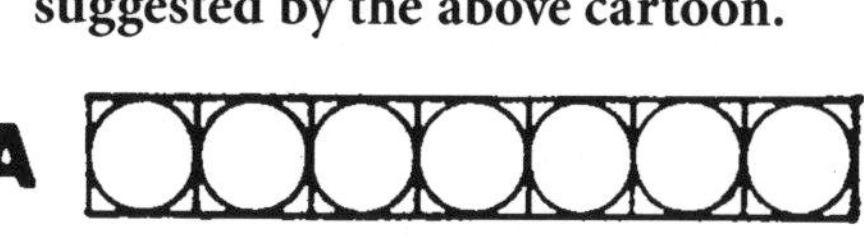

1972
PUZZLE
74

JUMBLE®

Unscramble these four Jumbles, one letter to each square, to form four ordinary words.

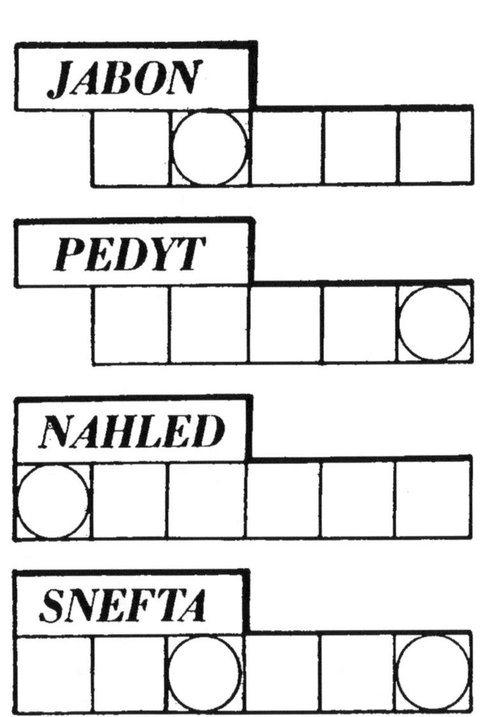
JABON
PEDYT
NAHLED
SNEFTA

Tonight again?
THEY SOMETIMES WORK AROUND THE CLOCK ON THE FARM.

Now arrange the circled letters to form the surprise answer, as suggested by the above cartoon.

Print answer here

1972 PUZZLE

75

JUMBLE®

Unscramble these four Jumbles, one letter to each square, to form four ordinary words.

ANUDT

PAMCH

SMIBUT

TINVER

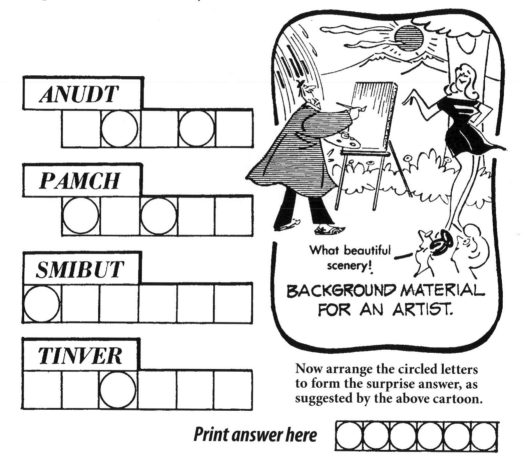

What beautiful scenery!

BACKGROUND MATERIAL FOR AN ARTIST.

Now arrange the circled letters to form the surprise answer, as suggested by the above cartoon.

Print answer here

1972
PUZZLE
76

JUMBLE®

Unscramble these four Jumbles, one letter to each square, to form four ordinary words.

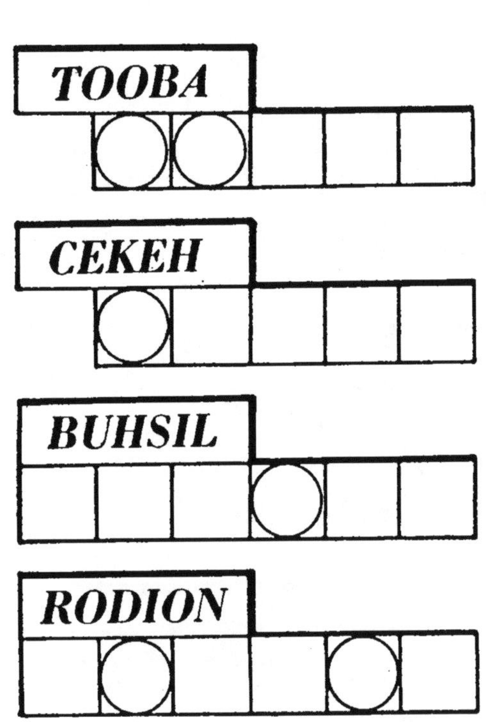
TOOBA
CEKEH
BUHSIL
RODION

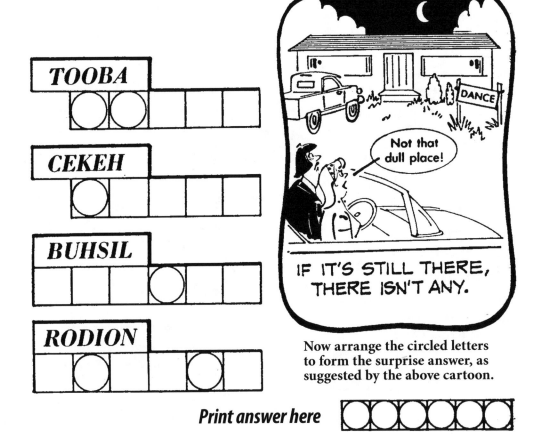

DANCE
Not that dull place!
IF IT'S STILL THERE, THERE ISN'T ANY.

Now arrange the circled letters to form the surprise answer, as suggested by the above cartoon.

Print answer here 

1972
PUZZLE
71

JUMBLE®

Unscramble these four Jumbles, one letter to each square, to form four ordinary words.

CRIHB
ANGLD
TROUCY
GLAARN
I gave at the office
Will you help?
THIS IS THE LEAST YOU CAN DO!

Now arrange the circled letters to form the surprise answer, as suggested by the above cartoon.

Print answer here

1972
PUZZLE
78

JUMBLE®

Unscramble these four Jumbles, one letter to each square, to form four ordinary words.

OCCIL

KYKIN

DAUSIN

QUAPEL

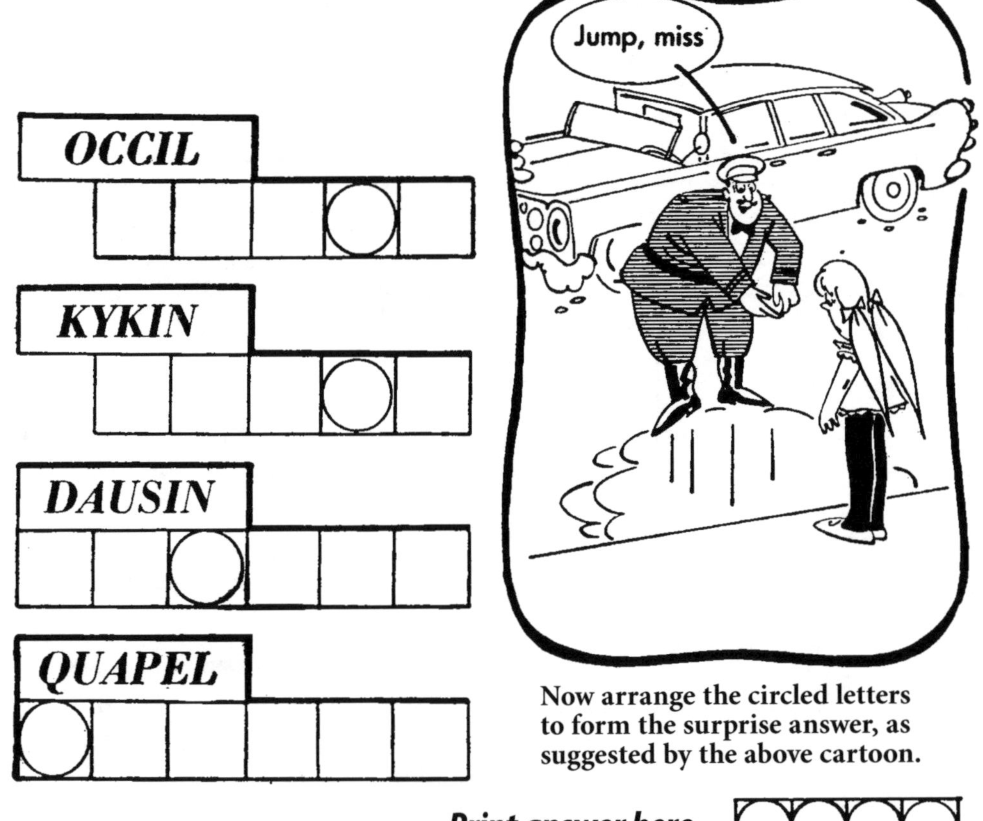
Jump, miss

Now arrange the circled letters to form the surprise answer, as suggested by the above cartoon.

Print answer here

1972
PUZZLE
79

JUMBLE®

Unscramble these four Jumbles, one letter to each square, to form four ordinary words.

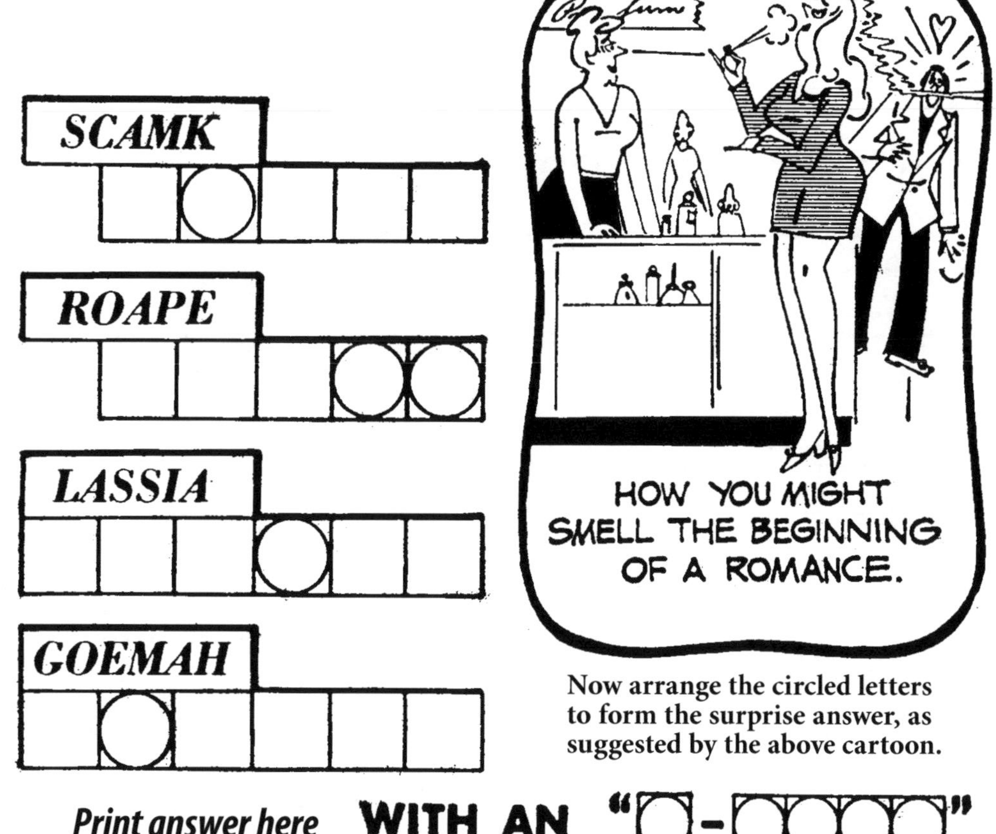
SCAMK
ROAPE
LASSIA
GOEMAH
HOW YOU MIGHT SMELL THE BEGINNING OF A ROMANCE.

Now arrange the circled letters to form the surprise answer, as suggested by the above cartoon.

Print answer here **WITH AN** "◯-◯◯◯◯"

1972
PUZZLE
80

JUMBLE®

Unscramble these four Jumbles, one letter to each square, to form four ordinary words.

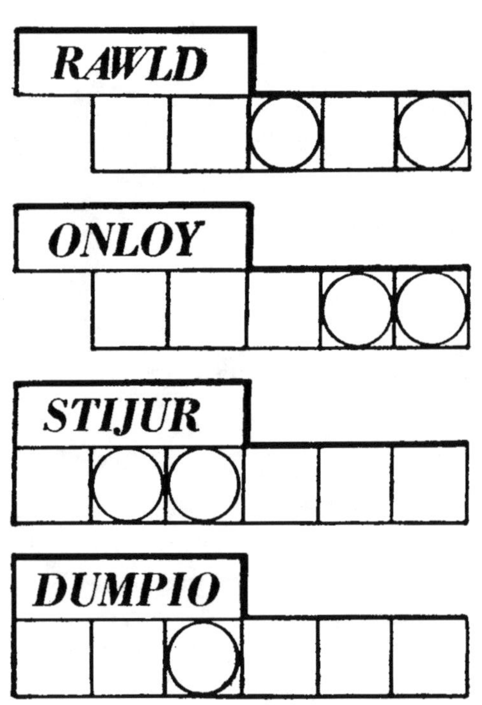
RAWLD
ONLOY
STIJUR
DUMPIO

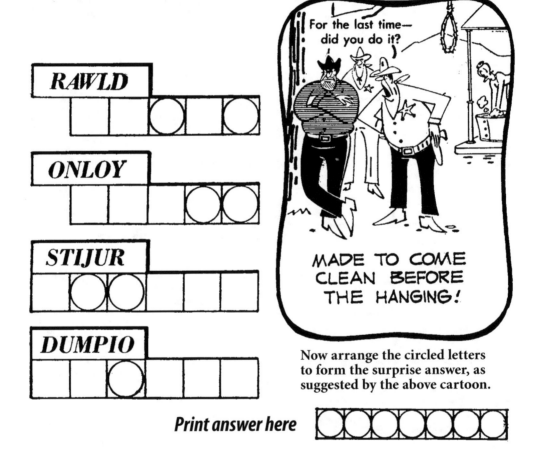

For the last time—did you do it?
MADE TO COME CLEAN BEFORE THE HANGING!

Now arrange the circled letters to form the surprise answer, as suggested by the above cartoon.

Print answer here 

1972
PUZZLE
81

JUMBLE®

Unscramble these four Jumbles, one letter to each square, to form four ordinary words.

SEGUS
YEMSS
MEUGLE
RAPPOL
Let him go. He's clean.
A
B
C
D
HE DECLARED—
HE WASN'T ONE!

Now arrange the circled letters to form the surprise answer, as suggested by the above cartoon.

Print answer here **A**

1972
PUZZLE
82

JUMBLE®

Unscramble these four Jumbles, one letter to each square, to form four ordinary words.

THONC

RESEA

PHOCON

NAIVED

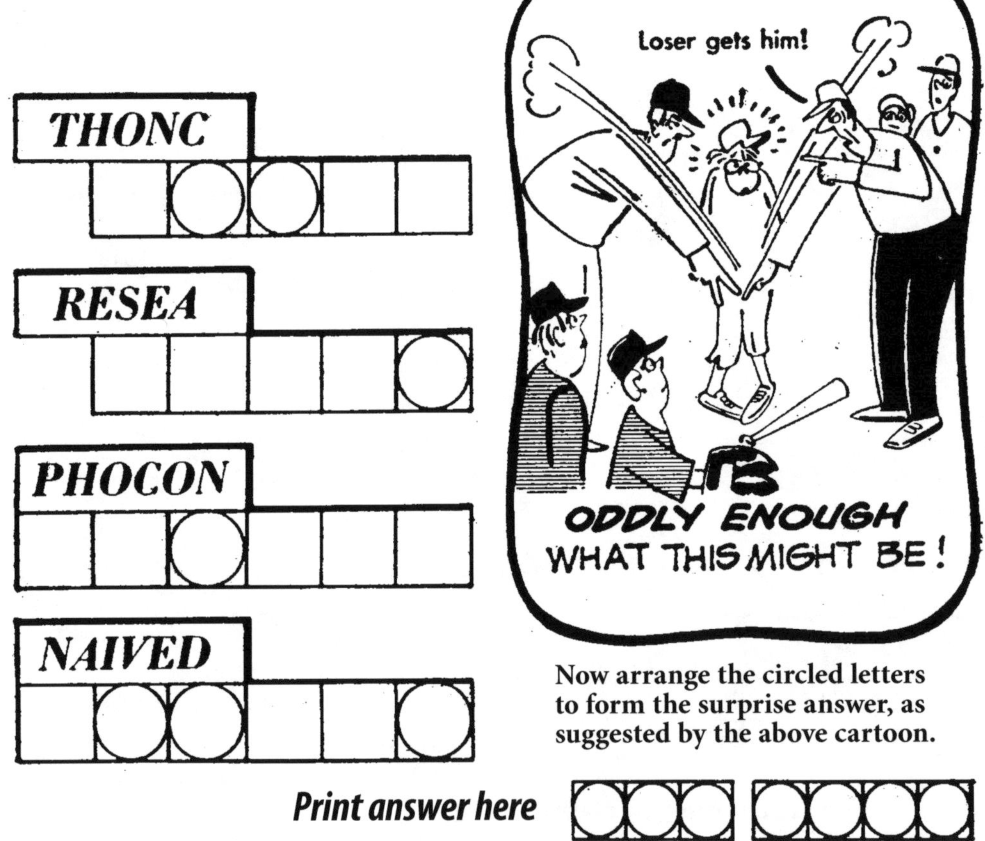
Loser gets him!
ODDLY ENOUGH WHAT THIS MIGHT BE!

Now arrange the circled letters to form the surprise answer, as suggested by the above cartoon.

Print answer here

1972 PUZZLE

83

JUMBLE®

Unscramble these four Jumbles, one letter to each square, to form four ordinary words.

SUMEO
TRIVE
MERRIP
PECILS
Say something off the top of your head
Who, me?
YOU WOULDN'T BE PREPARED TO MAKE SUCH A SPEECH!

Now arrange the circled letters to form the surprise answer, as suggested by the above cartoon.

Print answer here

1972
PUZZLE
84

JUMBLE®

Unscramble these four Jumbles, one letter to each square, to form four ordinary words.

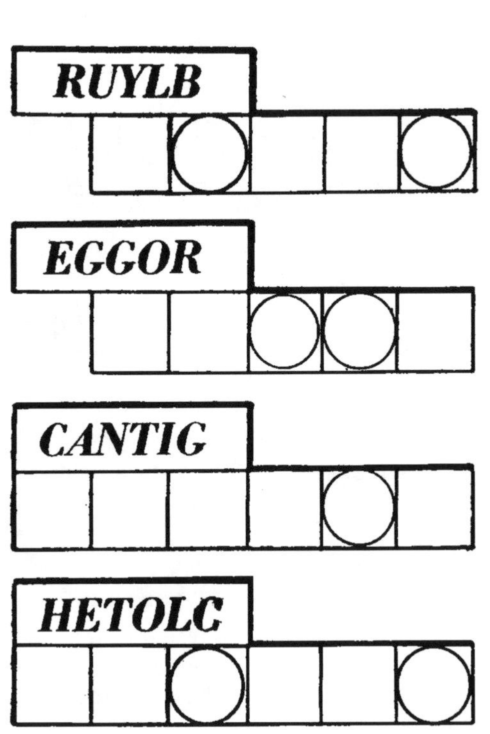
RUYLB
EGGOR
CANTIG
HETOLC

Not at your age!
for swingers
YOU CAN FEEL THIS BUT NOT GET IT!

Now arrange the circled letters to form the surprise answer, as suggested by the above cartoon.

Print answer here

1972
PUZZLE
85

JUMBLE®

Unscramble these four Jumbles, one letter to each square, to form four ordinary words.

MERIN

CRAFS

DORWYB

PENMAD

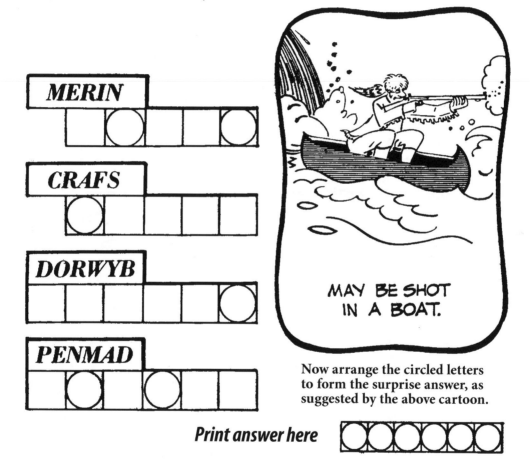

MAY BE SHOT
IN A BOAT.

Now arrange the circled letters to form the surprise answer, as suggested by the above cartoon.

Print answer here 

1972
PUZZLE
86

JUMBLE®

Unscramble these four Jumbles, one letter to each square, to form four ordinary words.

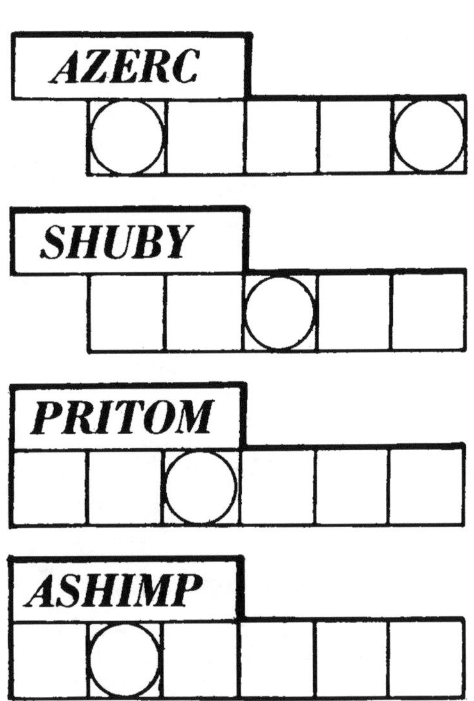
AZERC
SHUBY
PRITOM
ASHIMP

Boy—the way those gods carried on!
HOMER
YOU MIGHT FIND "SPICE" IN THESE POEMS.

Now arrange the circled letters to form the surprise answer, as suggested by the above cartoon.

Print answer here 

JUMBLE®

Unscramble these four Jumbles, one letter to each square, to form four ordinary words.

MALFE

HIKKA

DILEEY

LAFBLE

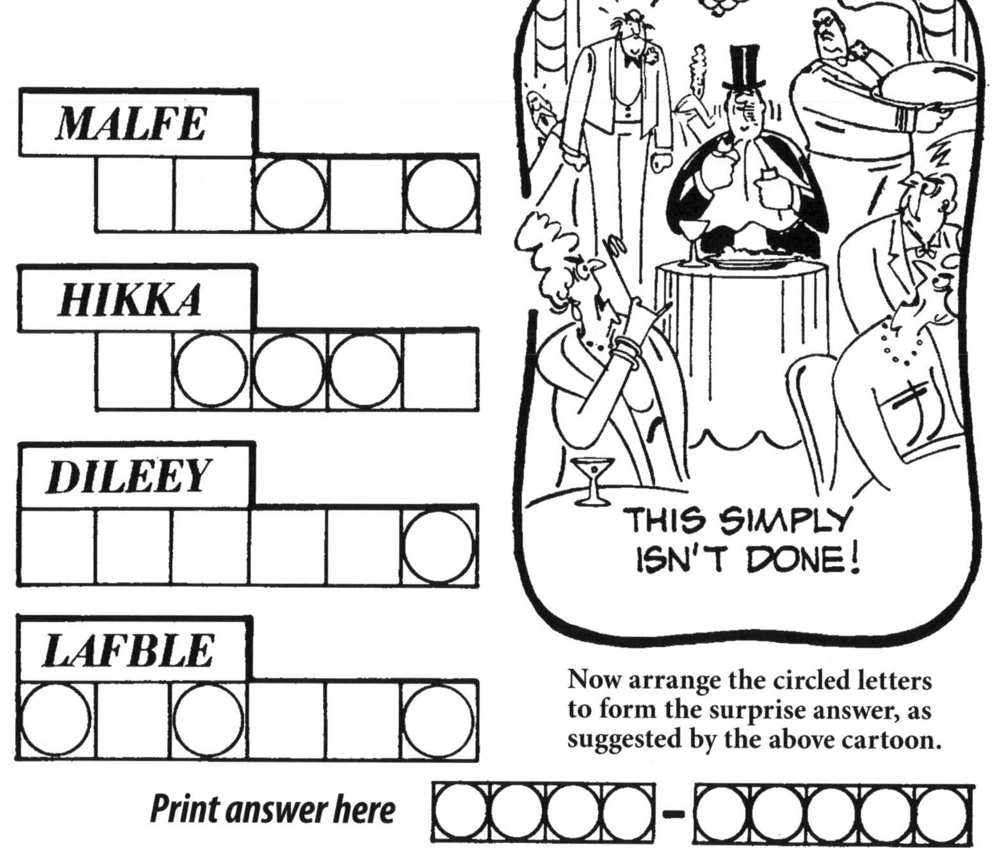
THIS SIMPLY ISN'T DONE!

Now arrange the circled letters to form the surprise answer, as suggested by the above cartoon.

Print answer here

1972
PUZZLE
88

JUMBLE®

Unscramble these four Jumbles, one letter to each square, to form four ordinary words.

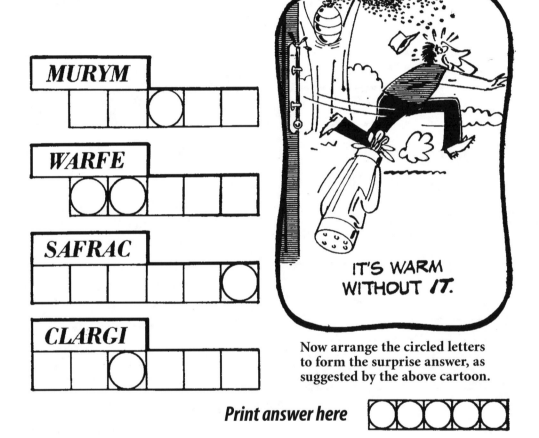

MURYM

WARFE

SAFRAC

CLARGI

IT'S WARM WITHOUT *IT.*

Now arrange the circled letters to form the surprise answer, as suggested by the above cartoon.

Print answer here

1972
PUZZLE
89

JUMBLE®

Unscramble these four Jumbles, one letter to each square, to form four ordinary words.

LYKIS

SURBT

FEEDAM

MALFEE

YAK
YAK
YAK
YAK
YAK
YAK
YAK
YAK
WHAT HE SUFFERED FROM ON A BORING DATE.

Now arrange the circled letters to form the surprise answer, as suggested by the above cartoon.

Print answer here "◯◯◯◯-◯◯◯◯◯"

1972
PUZZLE
90

JUMBLE®

Unscramble these four Jumbles, one letter to each square, to form four ordinary words.

YAARR

SOOME

INTADE

NARREB

Remember when you gave me this?
WHAT YOU COULD FIND IF YOU JUST OPENED THE DICTIONARY AT RANDOM.

Now arrange the circled letters to form the surprise answer, as suggested by the above cartoon.

Print answer here " "

1972 PUZZLE

91

JUMBLE®

Unscramble these four Jumbles, one letter to each square, to form four ordinary words.

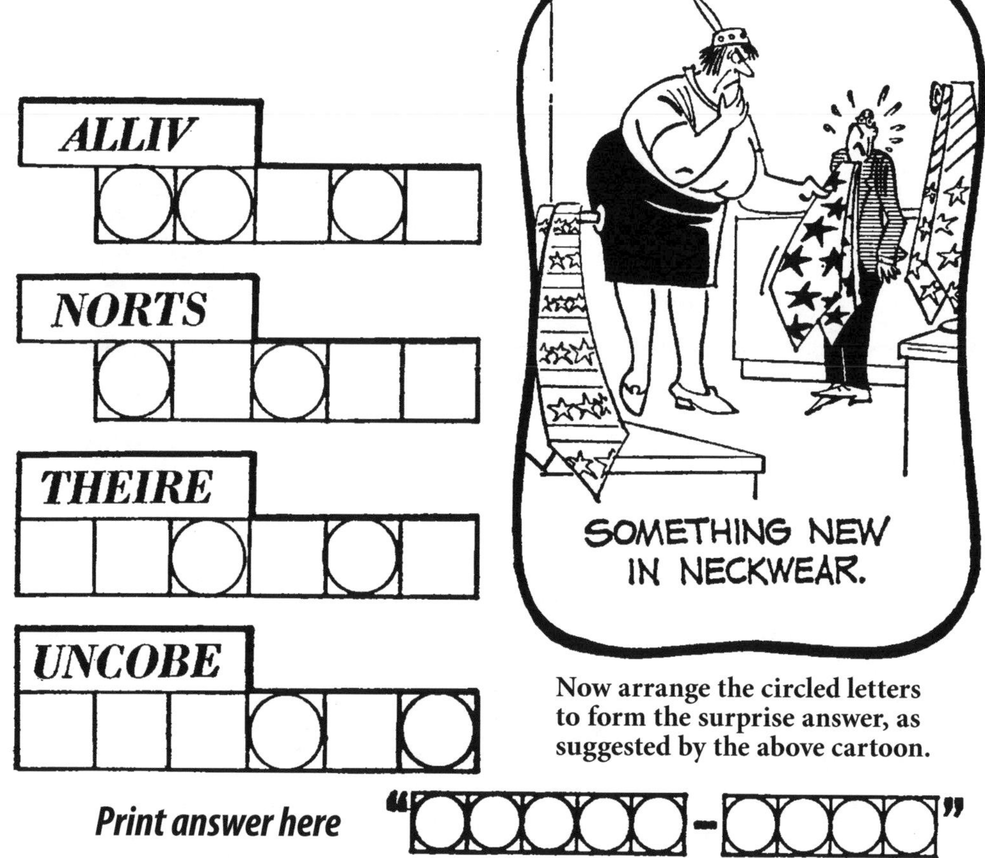
ALLIV
NORTS
THEIRE
UNCOBE
SOMETHING NEW IN NECKWEAR.

Now arrange the circled letters to form the surprise answer, as suggested by the above cartoon.

Print answer here "◯◯◯◯◯-◯◯◯◯"

1972
PUZZLE
92

JUMBLE®

Unscramble these four Jumbles, one letter to each square, to form four ordinary words.

MORGO

CHITH

GIRFID

FRAITY

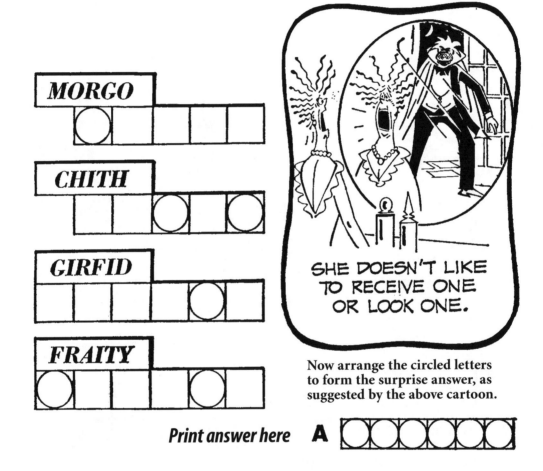

SHE DOESN'T LIKE TO RECEIVE ONE OR LOOK ONE.

Now arrange the circled letters to form the surprise answer, as suggested by the above cartoon.

Print answer here **A**

JUMBLE®

Unscramble these four Jumbles, one letter to each square, to form four ordinary words.

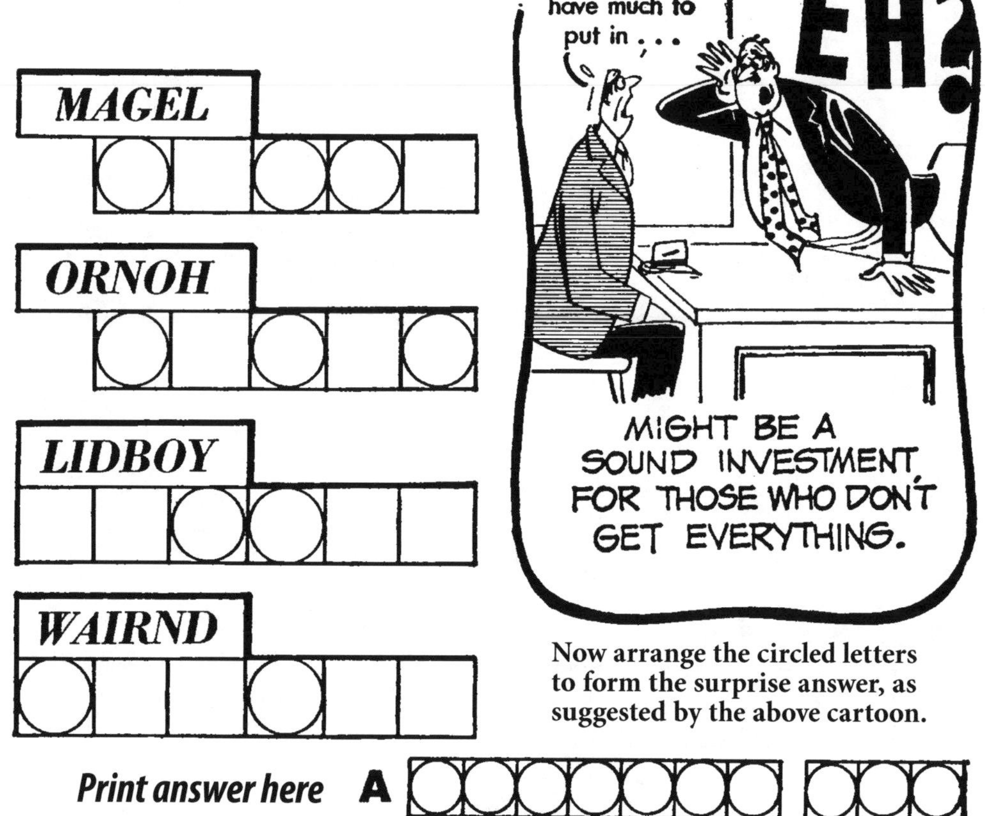
MAGEL
ORNOH
LIDBOY
WAIRND
Low pay . . . don't have much to put in . . .
EH?
MIGHT BE A SOUND INVESTMENT FOR THOSE WHO DON'T GET EVERYTHING.

Now arrange the circled letters to form the surprise answer, as suggested by the above cartoon.

Print answer here **A**

1972
PUZZLE
94

JUMBLE®

Unscramble these four Jumbles, one letter to each square, to form four ordinary words.

DARNB

ZEFOR

LOCASE

YARWIA

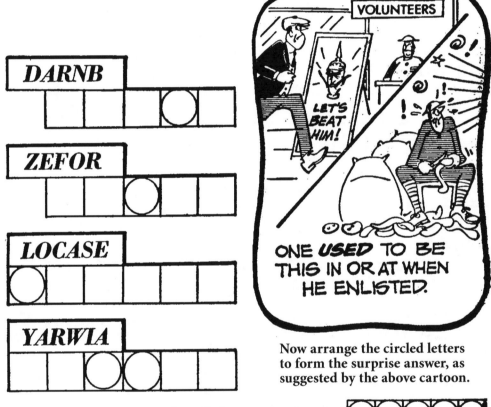

VOLUNTEERS
LET'S BEAT HIM!
ONE *USED* TO BE THIS IN OR AT WHEN HE ENLISTED.

Now arrange the circled letters to form the surprise answer, as suggested by the above cartoon.

Print answer here

1972
PUZZLE
95

JUMBLE®

Unscramble these four Jumbles, one letter to each square, to form four ordinary words.

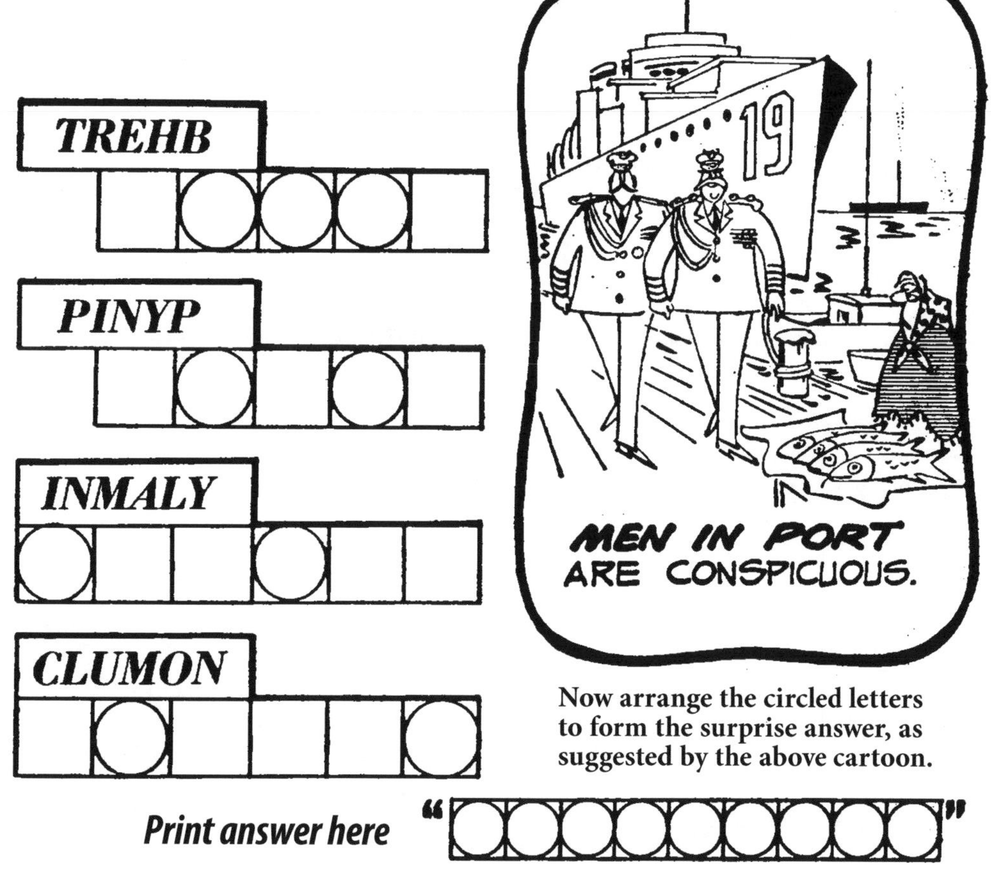
TREHB
PINYP
INMALY
CLUMON
MEN IN PORT ARE CONSPICUOUS.
Now arrange the circled letters to form the surprise answer, as suggested by the above cartoon.
Print answer here

1972
PUZZLE
96

JUMBLE®

Unscramble these four Jumbles, one letter to each square, to form four ordinary words.

HINEW

KARCC

UNDASE

REESHA

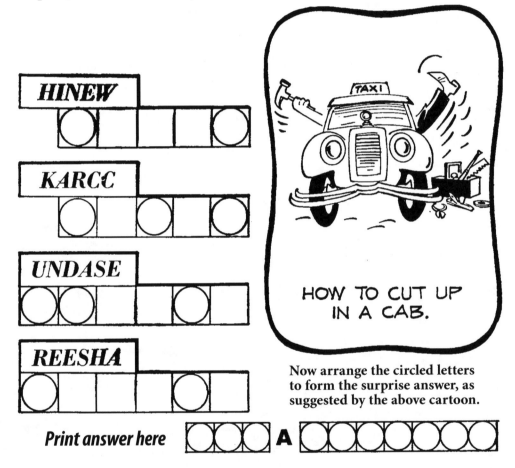

TAXI
HOW TO CUT UP IN A CAB.

Now arrange the circled letters to form the surprise answer, as suggested by the above cartoon.

Print answer here ◯◯◯ A ◯◯◯◯◯◯◯

JUMBLE®

Unscramble these four Jumbles, one letter to each square, to form four ordinary words.

GOUCH
HEANN
FRILCO
ENGOBY
Again in France?

Now arrange the circled letters to form the surprise answer, as suggested by the above cartoon.

Print answer here "○○○○○○"

1972
PUZZLE
98

JUMBLE®

Unscramble these four Jumbles, one letter to each square, to form four ordinary words.

ECHLE
MOBOL
GLENET
AMMBLE
BRIGADE HQS.
Lollipops for everybody!
SOUNDS LIKE A BIT OF A NUT IN THE ARMY.

Now arrange the circled letters to form the surprise answer, as suggested by the above cartoon.

Print answer here

1972
PUZZLE
99

JUMBLE®

Unscramble these four Jumbles, one letter to each square, to form four ordinary words.

PHACT

HIWSS

PIMAGE

GREJIG

SEVERAL IN
A FLIGHT.

Now arrange the circled letters to form the surprise answer, as suggested by the above cartoon.

Print answer here

1972
PUZZLE
100

JUMBLE®

Unscramble these four Jumbles, one letter to each square, to form four ordinary words.

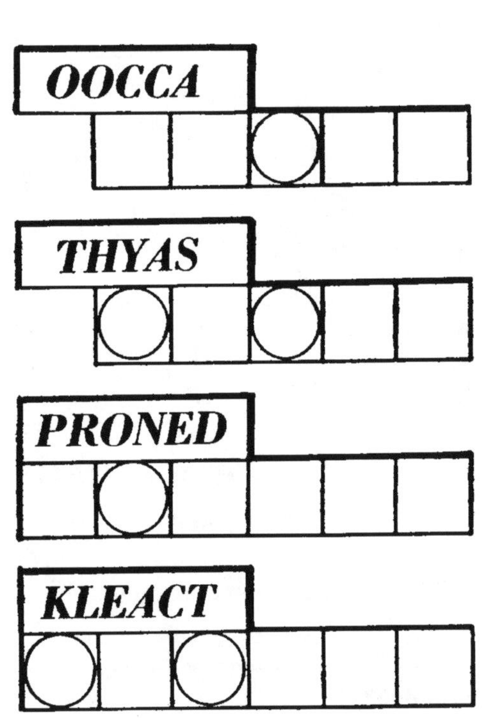
OOCCA
THYAS
PRONED
KLEACT

Have you heard the latest . . . ?
Drink up and shut up!
THIS DRINK MIGHT PUT AN END TO RUMORS.

Now arrange the circled letters to form the surprise answer, as suggested by the above cartoon.

Print answer here 

1972
PUZZLE
101

JUMBLE®

Unscramble these four Jumbles, one letter to each square, to form four ordinary words.

RAYIF

LOCON

UNNOIB

TREEMP

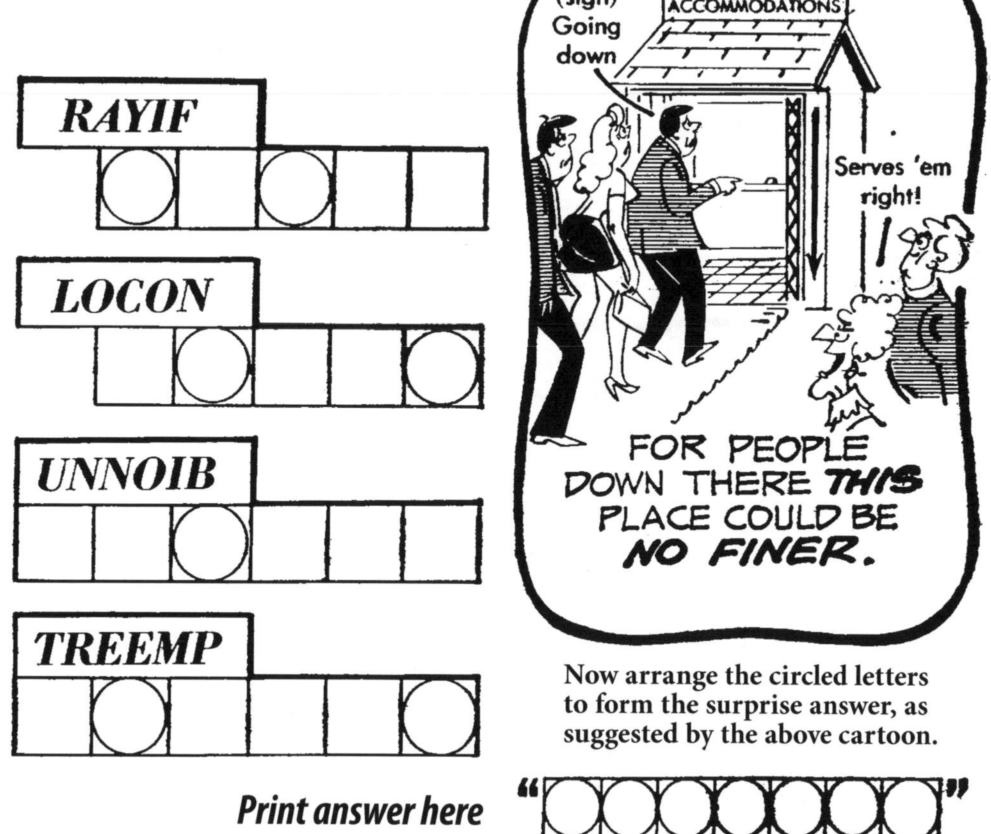
(sigh) Going down
ACCOMMODATIONS
Serves 'em right!
FOR PEOPLE DOWN THERE THIS PLACE COULD BE NO FINER.

Now arrange the circled letters to form the surprise answer, as suggested by the above cartoon.

Print answer here "　　　　　　　"

1972
PUZZLE
102

JUMBLE®

Unscramble these four Jumbles, one letter to each square, to form four ordinary words.

UGOBS
YERFO
TRYDAW
BOREEF
SOUNDS LIKE THIS CROOK ISN'T IN DANGER.

Now arrange the circled letters to form the surprise answer, as suggested by the above cartoon.

Print answer here A

1972 PUZZLE

103

JUMBLE®

Unscramble these four Jumbles, one letter to each square, to form four ordinary words.

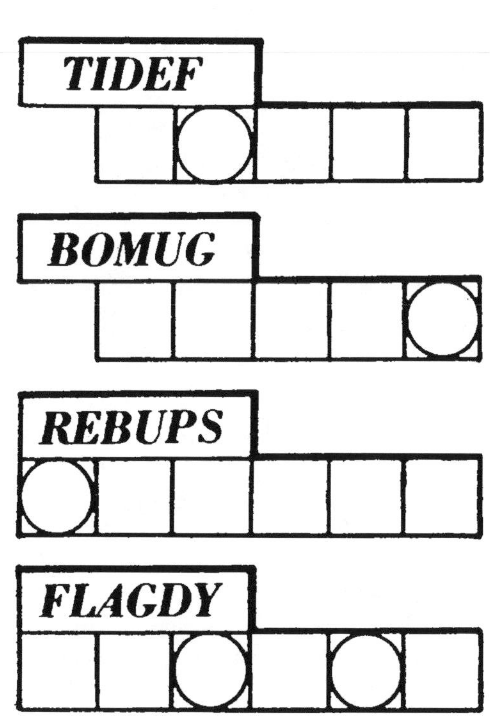

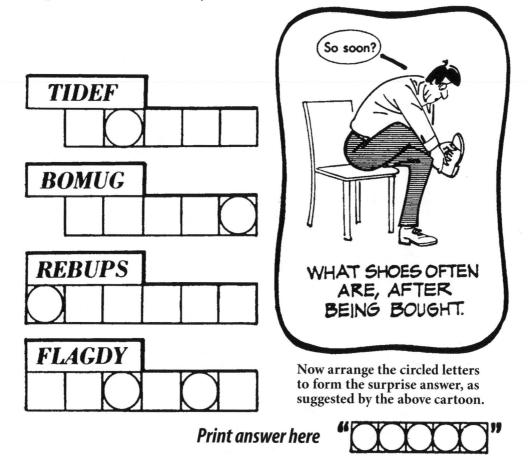

TIDEF
BOMUG
REBUPS
FLAGDY

So soon?
WHAT SHOES OFTEN ARE, AFTER BEING BOUGHT.

Now arrange the circled letters to form the surprise answer, as suggested by the above cartoon.

Print answer here 

1972
PUZZLE
104

JUMBLE®

Unscramble these four Jumbles, one letter to each square, to form four ordinary words.

HOALT

RADAW

TERRFE

LOSOCH

With this you'll really get the young chicks
HAIR PIECES
WHY A WIG CAN HELP YOU TO LIE ABOUT YOUR APPEARANCE.

Now arrange the circled letters to form the surprise answer, as suggested by the above cartoon.

Print answer here IT'S ◯ "◯◯◯◯◯◯ ◯◯◯◯◯"

1972 PUZZLE

105

JUMBLE®

Unscramble these four Jumbles, one letter to each square, to form four ordinary words.

YINNF
SMAUE
ACTOLE
TUKJEN
What kind do you use?
WE have a machine!
FOR DISHES
HARD ON THE HANDS!

Now arrange the circled letters to form the surprise answer, as suggested by the above cartoon.

Print answer here

1972
PUZZLE
106

JUMBLE®

Unscramble these four Jumbles, one letter to each square, to form four ordinary words.

TAALF

NATEE

GNININ

RISMEY

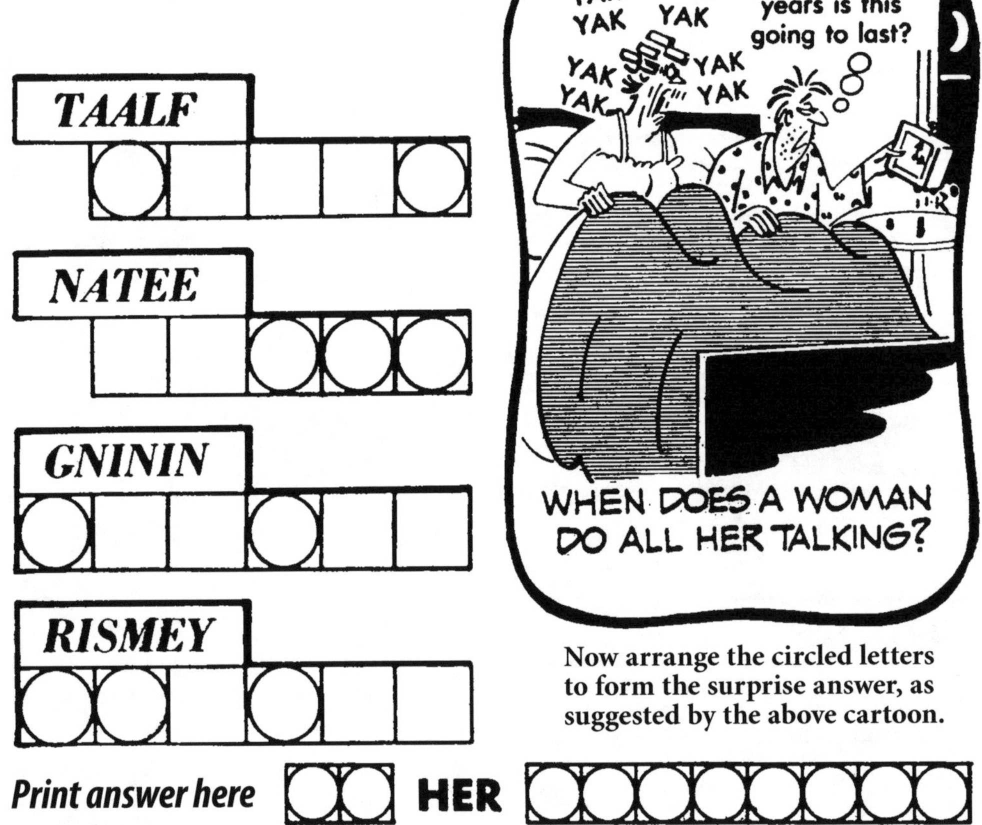
YAK YAK
YAK YAK
YAK YAK
YAK YAK
How many more years is this going to last?
WHEN DOES A WOMAN DO ALL HER TALKING?

Now arrange the circled letters to form the surprise answer, as suggested by the above cartoon.

Print answer here HER

1972
PUZZLE
107

JUMBLE®

Unscramble these four Jumbles, one letter to each square, to form four ordinary words.

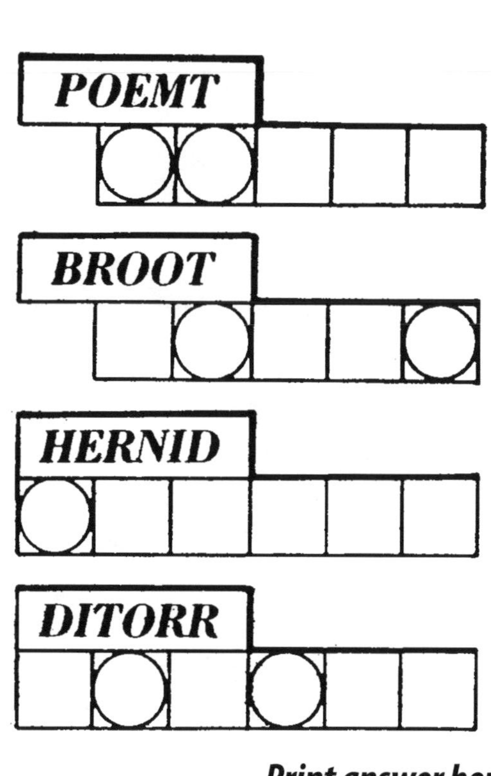
POEMT
BROOT
HERNID
DITORR

This is the life
SPREADS OUT UNDER A TREE.

Now arrange the circled letters to form the surprise answer, as suggested by the above cartoon.

Print answer here

1972
PUZZLE
108

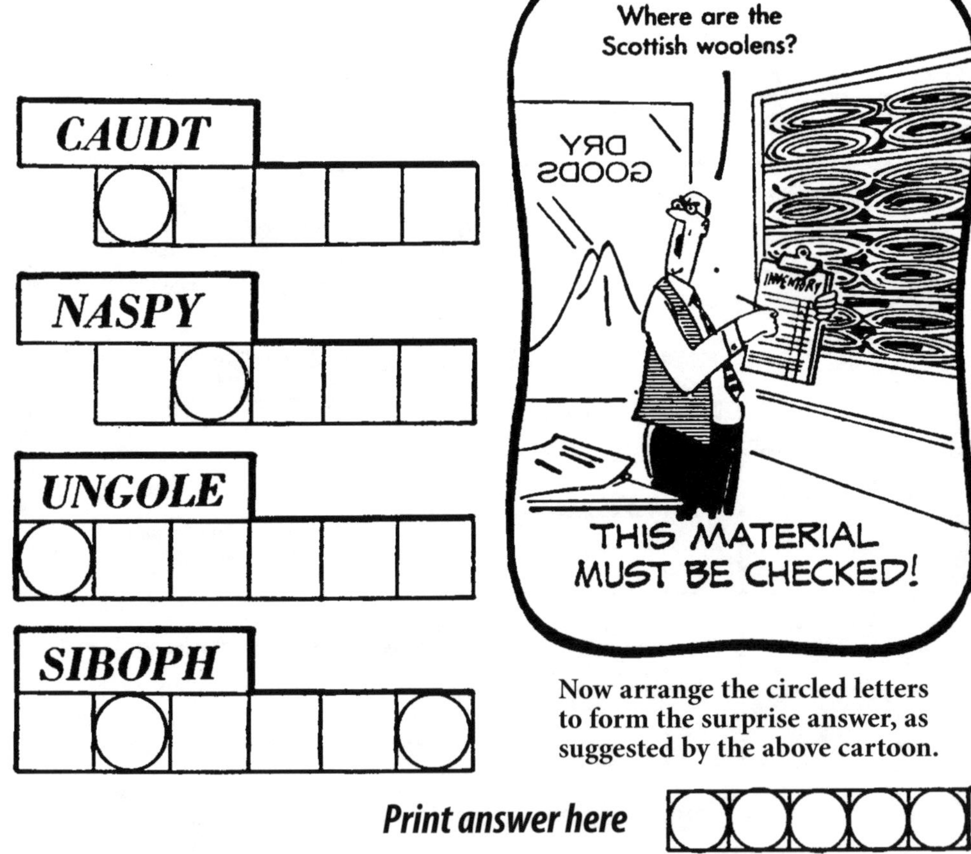
JUMBLE
Unscramble these four Jumbles, one letter to each square, to form four ordinary words.
CAUDT
NASPY
UNGOLE
SIBOPH
Where are the Scottish woolens?
DRY GOODS
INVENTORY
THIS MATERIAL MUST BE CHECKED!
Now arrange the circled letters to form the surprise answer, as suggested by the above cartoon.

Print answer here

1972
PUZZLE
109

JUMBLE®

Unscramble these four Jumbles, one letter to each square, to form four ordinary words.

ENSOO
BELLI
LETHAH
GANNIA
Wait'll you see OUR kid
CHILD PRODIGY NIGHT
Bar
THEY SHOW SIGNS OF BRILLIANCE.
Now arrange the circled letters to form the surprise answer, as suggested by the above cartoon.
Print answer here

1972
PUZZLE
110

JUMBLE®

Unscramble these four Jumbles, one letter to each square, to form four ordinary words.

VERIP

MYLAD

COLOTE

HYNDIG

Yes, but what's he done lately?
WHAT AN UNEMPLOYED FILM STAR IS.

Now arrange the circled letters to form the surprise answer, as suggested by the above cartoon.

Print answer here **A**

1972
PUZZLE
111

JUMBLE®

Unscramble these four Jumbles, one letter to each square, to form four ordinary words.

ACEEP

HAFFC

TONPHY

LAVOAW

Is it tender?
Very!
THIS BIRD HAS HIS HAT ON!

Now arrange the circled letters to form the surprise answer, as suggested by the above cartoon.

Print answer here A "◯◯◯-◯◯"

1972
PUZZLE
112

JUMBLE®

Unscramble these four Jumbles, one letter to each square, to form four ordinary words.

EUQUE

POAKK

SLAQUL

ROTGOT

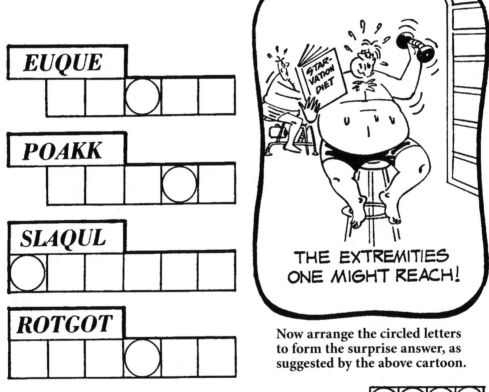

THE EXTREMITIES ONE MIGHT REACH!

Now arrange the circled letters to form the surprise answer, as suggested by the above cartoon.

Print answer here

JUMBLE®

Unscramble these four Jumbles, one letter to each square, to form four ordinary words.

NEVAK
SACEE
TESVIN
MESTIK
How high?
With snow, it's higher
THEY CONTAIN MORE FEET IN WINTER THAN IN SUMMER.

Now arrange the circled letters to form the surprise answer, as suggested by the above cartoon.

Print answer here

1972
PUZZLE
114

JUMBLE®

Unscramble these four Jumbles, one letter to each square, to form four ordinary words.

SWEHL

YACKT

FALOTA

DUBUSE

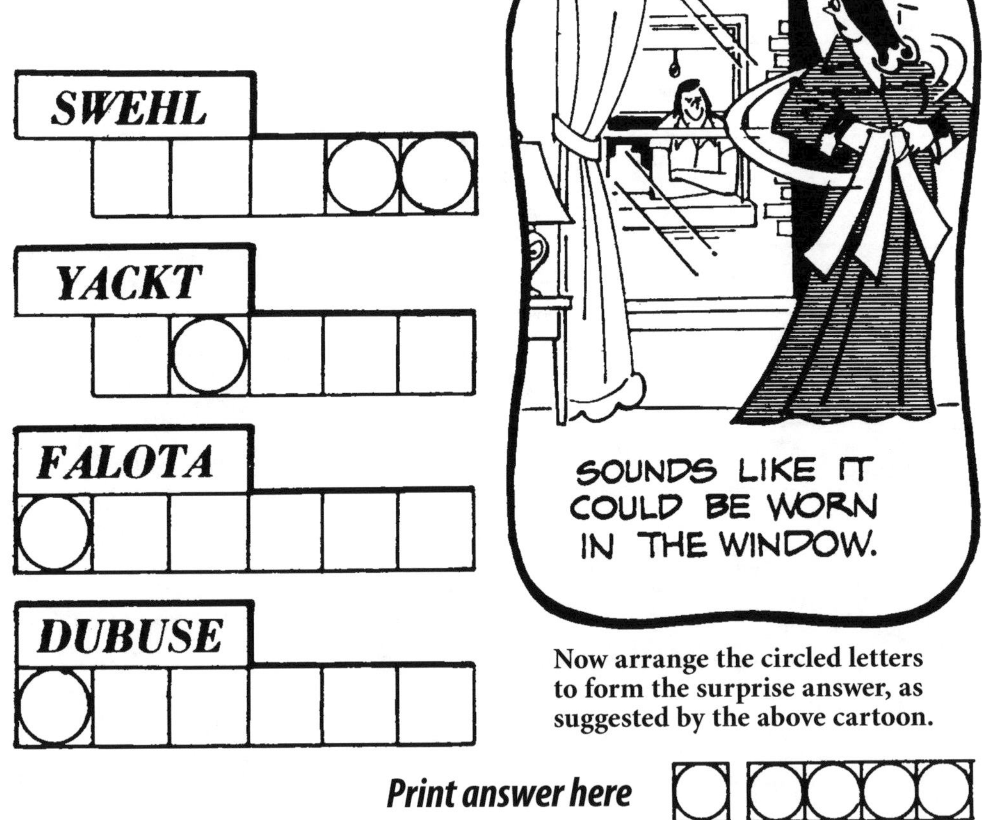
SOUNDS LIKE IT COULD BE WORN IN THE WINDOW.

Now arrange the circled letters to form the surprise answer, as suggested by the above cartoon.

Print answer here

1972
PUZZLE
115

JUMBLE®

Unscramble these four Jumbles, one letter to each square, to form four ordinary words.

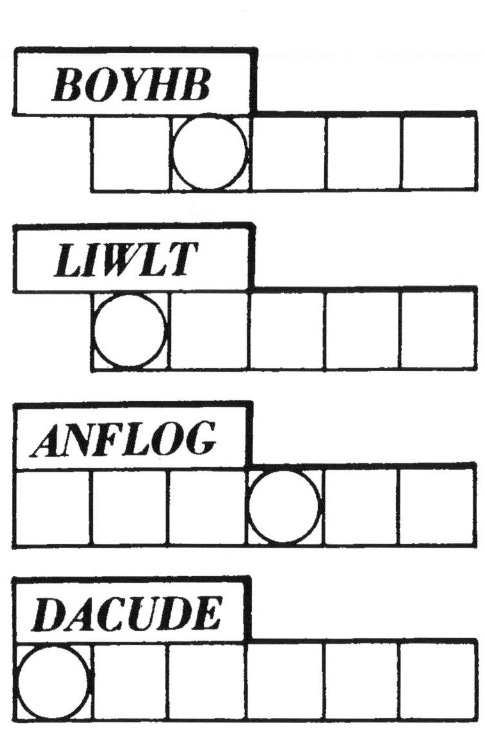
BOYHB
LIWLT
ANFLOG
DACUDE

Love this spread!
Billy ate my can of beans!
A KIND OF BUTTER THAT'S SPELLED WITH FOUR LETTERS.

Now arrange the circled letters to form the surprise answer, as suggested by the above cartoon.

Print answer here

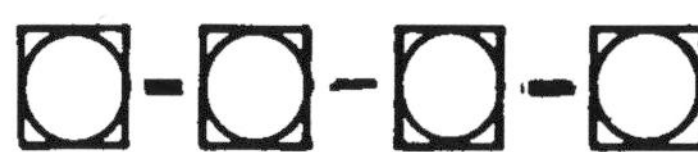

1972
PUZZLE
116

JUMBLE®

Unscramble these four Jumbles, one letter to each square, to form four ordinary words.

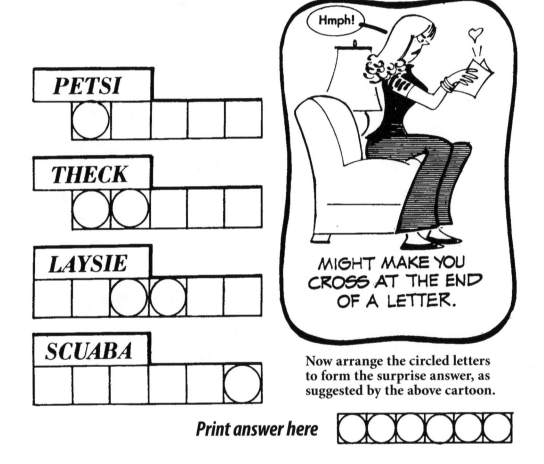

PETSI
THECK
LAYSIE
SCUABA
Hmph!
MIGHT MAKE YOU CROSS AT THE END OF A LETTER.

Now arrange the circled letters to form the surprise answer, as suggested by the above cartoon.

Print answer here

1972
PUZZLE
117

JUMBLE®

Unscramble these four Jumbles, one letter to each square, to form four ordinary words.

DEEXU

ANAUF

CERUDE

LAAXYG

Give!
I'm inclined . . .
THIS COULD MAKE YOU FEEL YOU OUGHT TO DO SOMETHING.

Now arrange the circled letters to form the surprise answer, as suggested by the above cartoon.

Print answer here

1972
PUZZLE
118

JUMBLE®

Unscramble these four Jumbles, one letter to each square, to form four ordinary words.

TACCH

ERRAM

THYROW

LAUTES

I'm prepared
SHELTER
MAY HELP PREVENT AN INVASION BY AIR.

Now arrange the circled letters to form the surprise answer, as suggested by the above cartoon.

Print answer here A

1972
PUZZLE
119

JUMBLE®

Unscramble these four Jumbles, one letter to each square, to form four ordinary words.

NAKTE

BYNAD

SOTILD

DELTUC

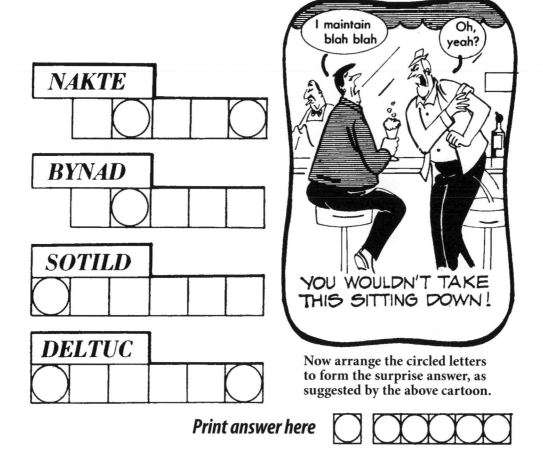

I maintain blah blah
Oh, yeah?

YOU WOULDN'T TAKE THIS SITTING DOWN!

Now arrange the circled letters to form the surprise answer, as suggested by the above cartoon.

Print answer here

1972
PUZZLE
120

JUMBLE®

Unscramble these four Jumbles, one letter to each square, to form four ordinary words.

NORDE

COVAL

TAFLEY

HALINE

Oops—sorry!
IT SHOULD BE PUT BACK ON ITS COURSE.

Now arrange the circled letters to form the surprise answer, as suggested by the above cartoon.

Print answer here

1972 PUZZLE 121

JUMBLE®

Unscramble these four Jumbles, one letter to each square, to form four ordinary words.

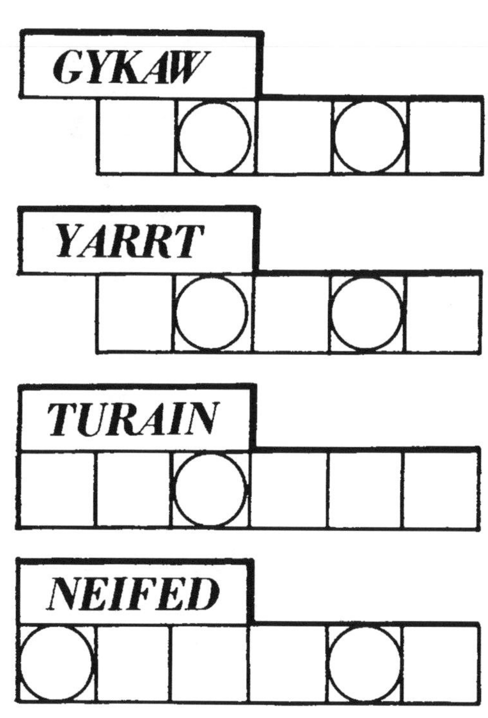
GYKAW
YARRT
TURAIN
NEIFED

PUB
THE FIRST PART IS RATHER HEAVY, BUT THE WHOLE CAN BE LIFTED EASILY— AND WILLINGLY!

Now arrange the circled letters to form the surprise answer, as suggested by the above cartoon.

Print answer here A "

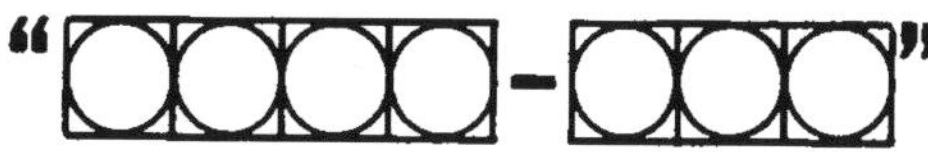
"

1972
PUZZLE
122

JUMBLE®

Unscramble these four Jumbles, one letter to each square, to form four ordinary words.

THILE

ZIPER

BLAURT

CLOAJE

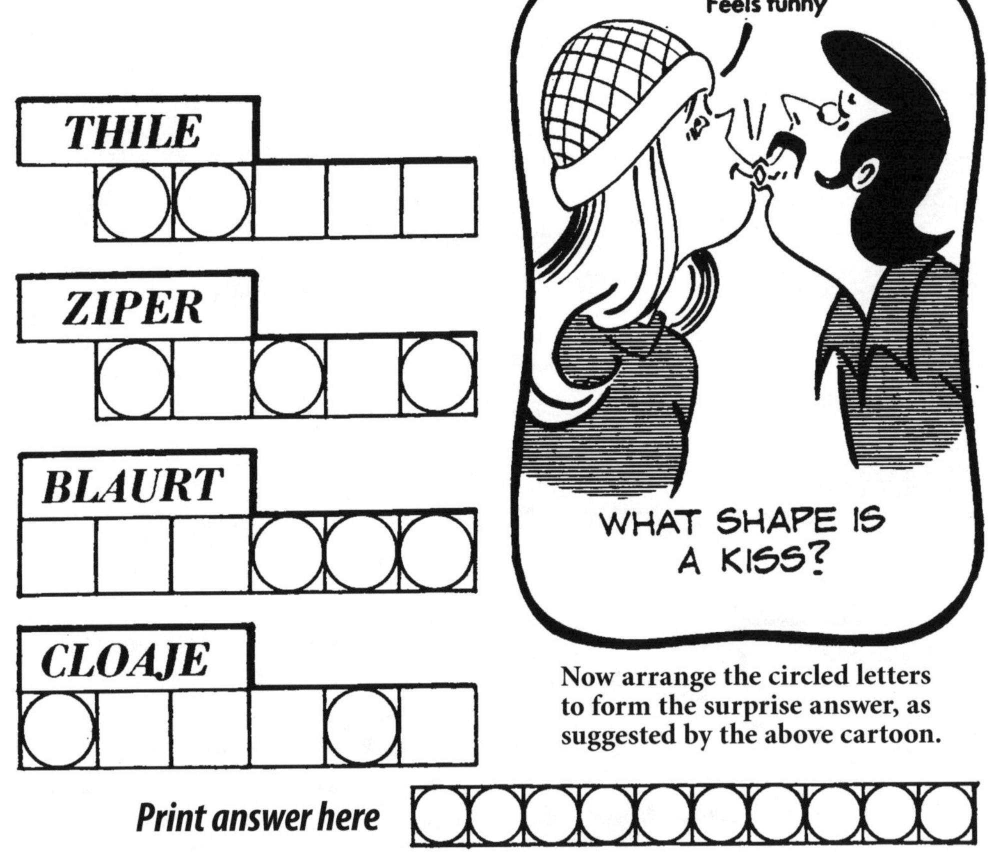
Feels funny
WHAT SHAPE IS A KISS?

Now arrange the circled letters to form the surprise answer, as suggested by the above cartoon.

Print answer here

1972
PUZZLE
123

JUMBLE®

Unscramble these four Jumbles, one letter to each square, to form four ordinary words.

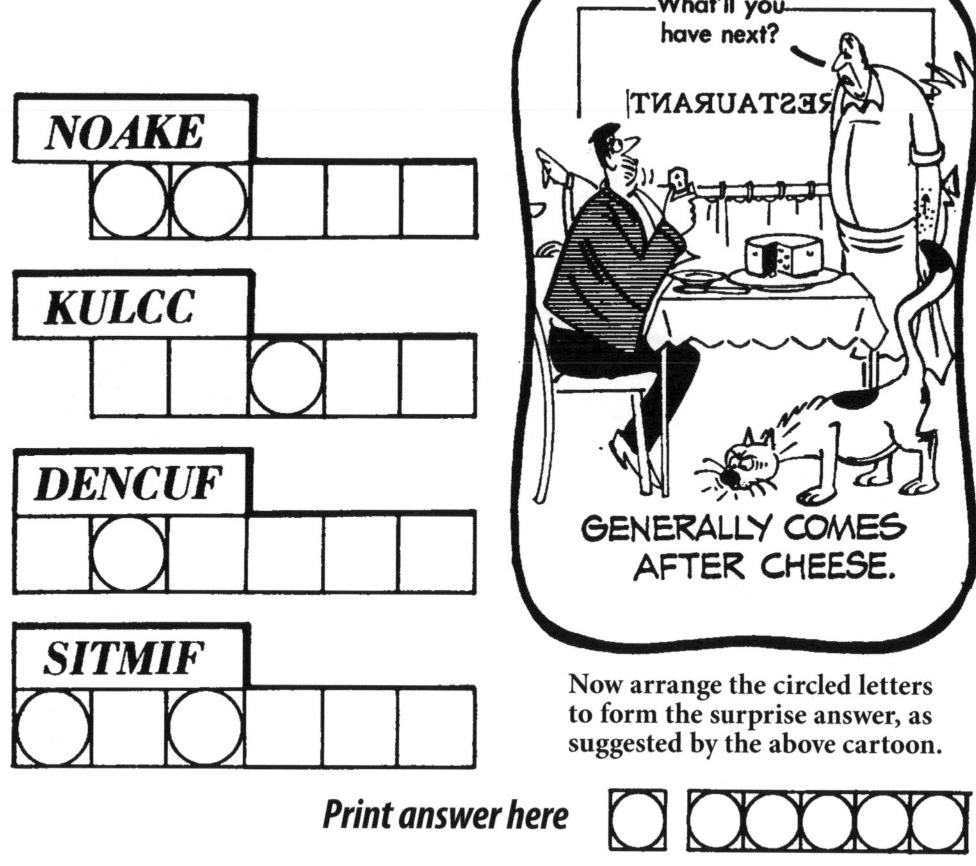
NOAKE
KULCC
DENCUF
SITMIF
What'll you have next?
RESTAURANT
GENERALLY COMES AFTER CHEESE.
Now arrange the circled letters to form the surprise answer, as suggested by the above cartoon.
Print answer here

1972
PUZZLE
124

JUMBLE®

Unscramble these four Jumbles, one letter to each square, to form four ordinary words.

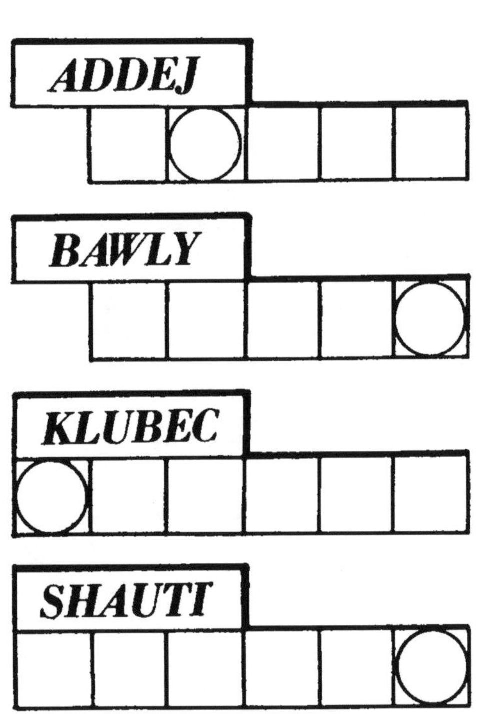
ADDEJ
BAWLY
KLUBEC
SHAUTI

This'll flush out the remainder
A MOPPING-UP OPERATION BY THE NAVY.

Now arrange the circled letters to form the surprise answer, as suggested by the above cartoon.

Print answer here

1972
PUZZLE
125

JUMBLE®

Unscramble these four Jumbles, one letter to each square, to form four ordinary words.

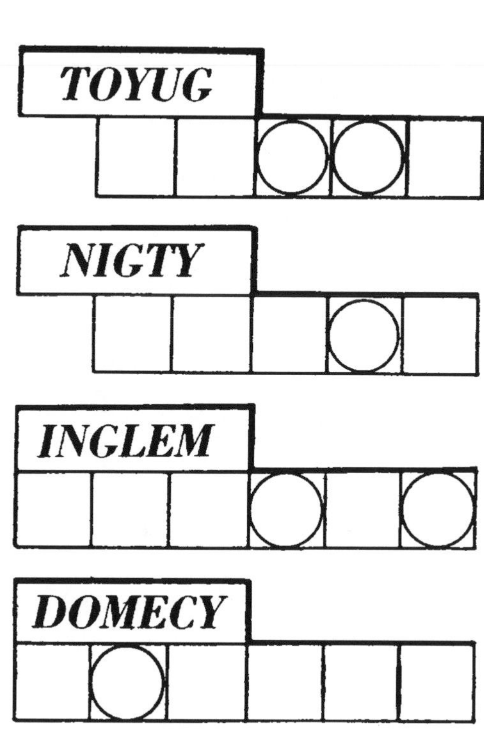
TOYUG
NIGTY
INGLEM
DOMECY

I submit this as Exhibit A
Keen!
OFTEN GROWS SHARPER WITH USE.

Now arrange the circled letters to form the surprise answer, as suggested by the above cartoon.

Print answer here A

1972
PUZZLE
126

JUMBLE®

Unscramble these four Jumbles, one letter to each square, to form four ordinary words.

MAUCS
NOPER
YAVINT
TANIAT
Wait'll he REALLY gets going!
THIS RUSSIAN HAS FOUR TO START WITH!

Now arrange the circled letters to form the surprise answer, as suggested by the above cartoon.

Print answer here

JUMBLE®

Unscramble these four Jumbles, one letter to each square, to form four ordinary words.

LUGEY

PYJUM

MASHAT

HARDIS

She's a gem and much rarer than the mother of her

Now arrange the circled letters to form the surprise answer, as suggested by the above cartoon.

Print answer here " "

1972
PUZZLE
128

JUMBLE®

Unscramble these four Jumbles, one letter to each square, to form four ordinary words.

TUBOA

GERAW

TIPMER

LYKING

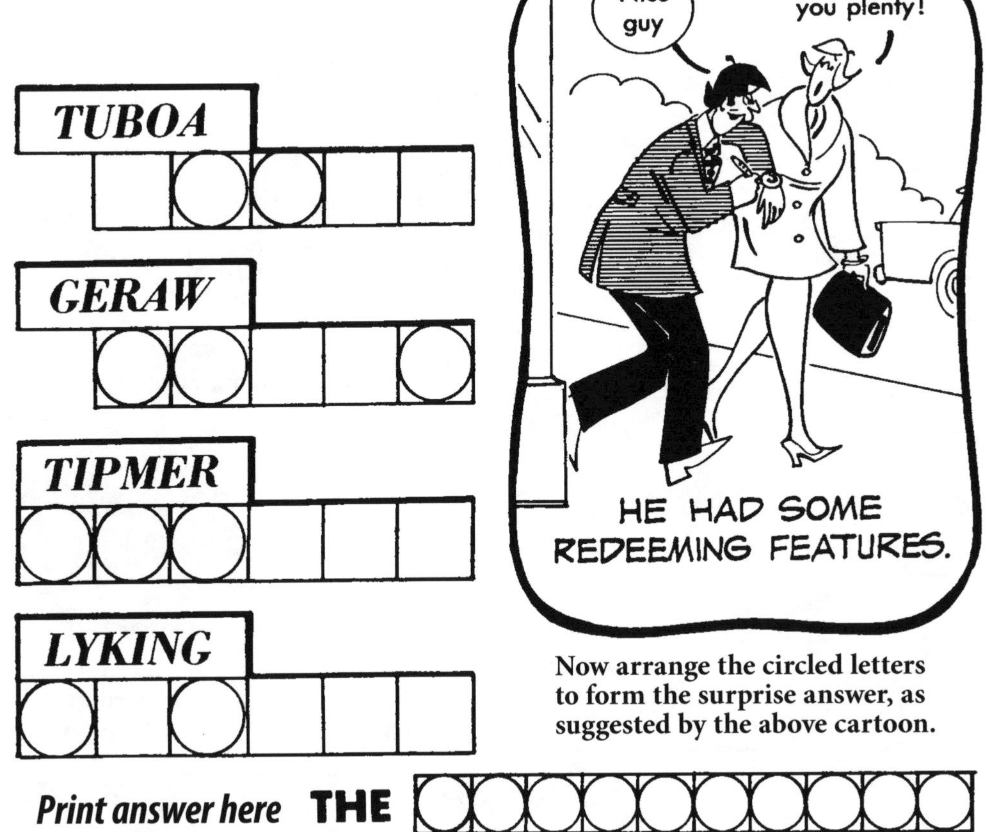
Nice guy
But it cost you plenty!
HE HAD SOME REDEEMING FEATURES.

Now arrange the circled letters to form the surprise answer, as suggested by the above cartoon.

Print answer here **THE**

1972 PUZZLE

129

JUMBLE®

Unscramble these four Jumbles, one letter to each square, to form four ordinary words.

VALEE
BOANT
SNULES
CATBUD
HOW TO COMPLAIN ABOUT A DULL KNIFE.

Now arrange the circled letters to form the surprise answer, as suggested by the above cartoon.

Print answer here

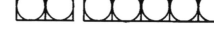

1972
PUZZLE
130

JUMBLE®

Unscramble these four Jumbles, one letter to each square, to form four ordinary words.

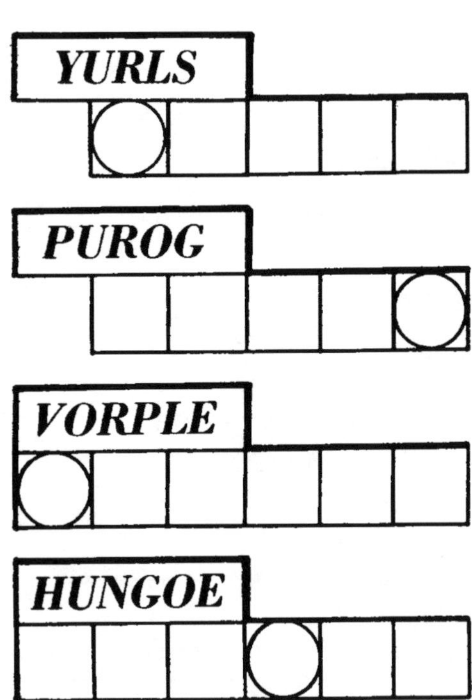
YURLS
PUROG
VORPLE
HUNGOE

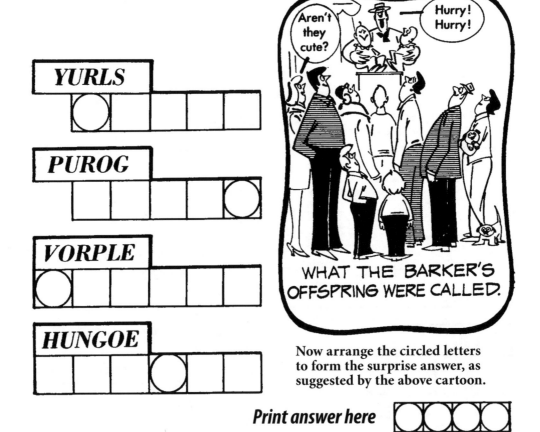

Aren't they cute?
Hurry! Hurry!
WHAT THE BARKER'S OFFSPRING WERE CALLED.

Now arrange the circled letters to form the surprise answer, as suggested by the above cartoon.

Print answer here 

1972 PUZZLE 131

JUMBLE®

Unscramble these four Jumbles, one letter to each square, to form four ordinary words.

ORRMA

HACOP

PRUMAK

REESIO

This stuff is mine!
COULD BE A USELESS THING— TO FIGHT OVER!

Now arrange the circled letters to form the surprise answer, as suggested by the above cartoon.

Print answer here

1972
PUZZLE
132

JUMBLE®

Unscramble these four Jumbles, one letter to each square, to form four ordinary words.

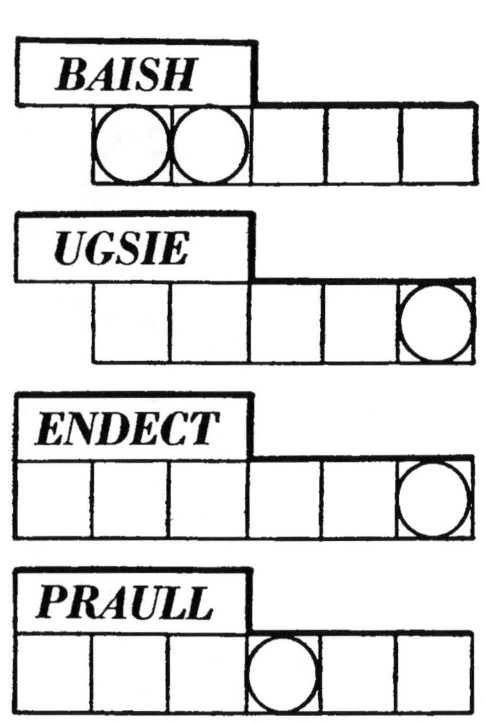
BAISH
UGSIE
ENDECT
PRAULL

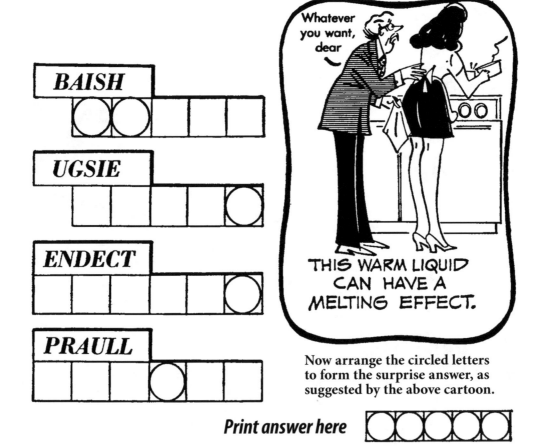

Whatever you want, dear
THIS WARM LIQUID CAN HAVE A MELTING EFFECT.

Now arrange the circled letters to form the surprise answer, as suggested by the above cartoon.

Print answer here

1972
PUZZLE
133

JUMBLE®

Unscramble these four Jumbles, one letter to each square, to form four ordinary words.

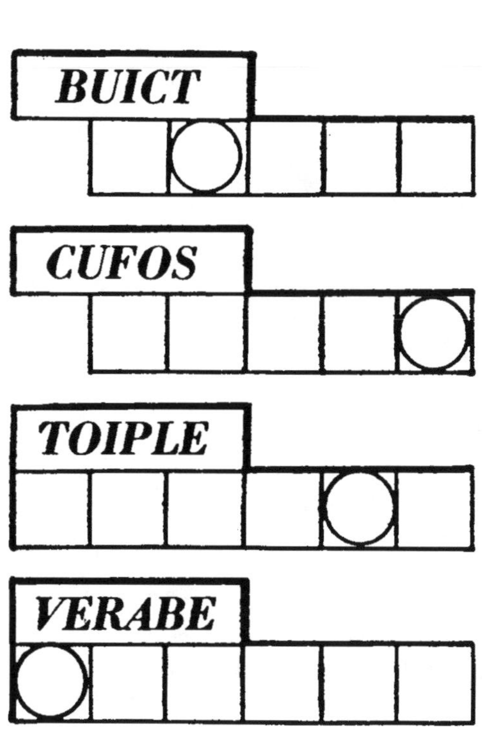

BUICT
CUFOS
TOIPLE
VERABE

I maintain...
On the contrary...
THERE MAY BE OBJECTIONS INVOLVED IN THE USE OF THESE WORDS!

Now arrange the circled letters to form the surprise answer, as suggested by the above cartoon.

Print answer here

1972
PUZZLE
134

JUMBLE®

Unscramble these four Jumbles, one letter to each square, to form four ordinary words.

NITHK

POAYS

ABLEED

DEFILD

Must be nails in your shoe!
BOOTS

Now arrange the circled letters to form the surprise answer, as suggested by the above cartoon.

Print answer here " "

1972
PUZZLE
135

JUMBLE®

Unscramble these four Jumbles, one letter to each square, to form four ordinary words.

SOSAB
HUVOC
EVIDID
LOYMED
ROOFING CO.
"DROPPED" BY A NOSY PERSON.

Now arrange the circled letters to form the surprise answer, as suggested by the above cartoon.

Print answer here " "

1972
PUZZLE
136

JUMBLE®

Unscramble these four Jumbles, one letter to each square, to form four ordinary words.

RAMEF

GREBA

LAMORN

RUMMUR

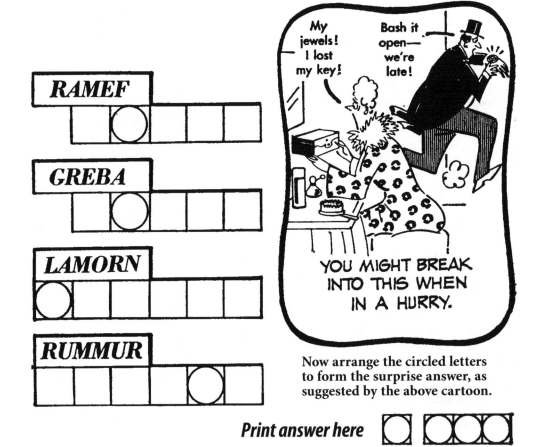

My jewels! I lost my key!
Bash it open— we're late!
YOU MIGHT BREAK INTO THIS WHEN IN A HURRY.

Now arrange the circled letters to form the surprise answer, as suggested by the above cartoon.

Print answer here

1972 PUZZLE

137

JUMBLE®

Unscramble these four Jumbles, one letter to each square, to form four ordinary words.

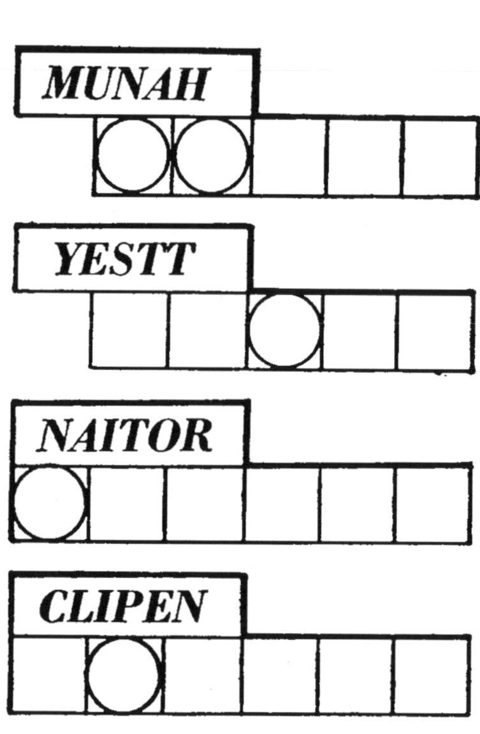
MUNAH
YESTT
NAITOR
CLIPEN

Could connect us with that woman!

Now arrange the circled letters to form the surprise answer, as suggested by the above cartoon.

Print answer here

1972
PUZZLE
138

JUMBLE®

Unscramble these four Jumbles, one letter to each square, to form four ordinary words.

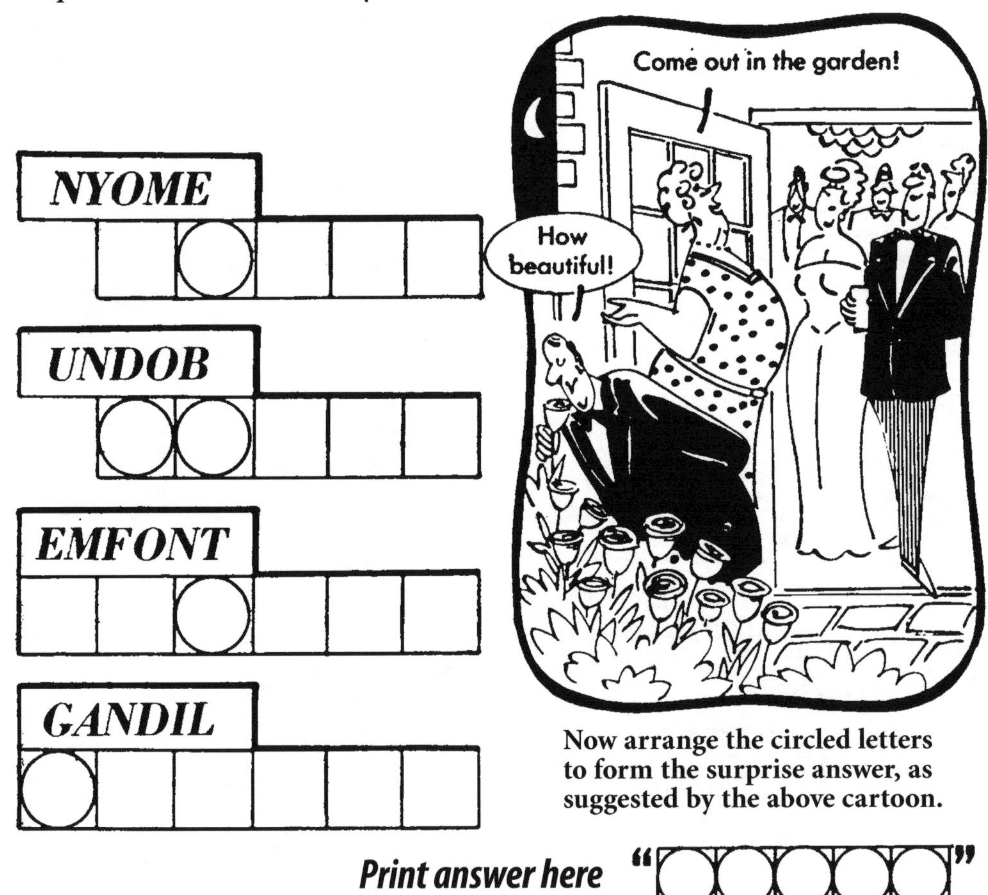
NYOME
UNDOB
EMFONT
GANDIL
Come out in the garden!
How beautiful!

Now arrange the circled letters to form the surprise answer, as suggested by the above cartoon.

Print answer here “◯◯◯◯◯”

1972
PUZZLE
139

JUMBLE®

Unscramble these four Jumbles, one letter to each square, to form four ordinary words.

YORFT

ARBIN

HIMSUL

ROPOLY

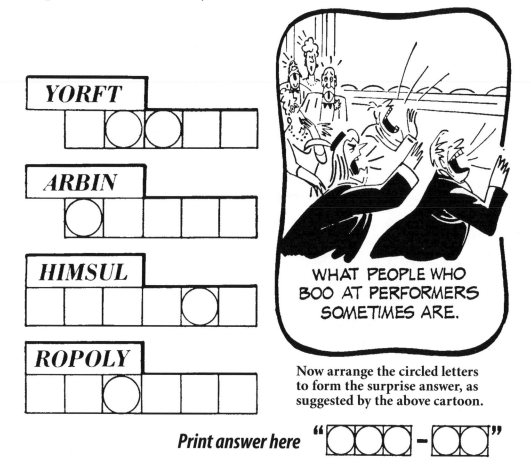

WHAT PEOPLE WHO BOO AT PERFORMERS SOMETIMES ARE.

Now arrange the circled letters to form the surprise answer, as suggested by the above cartoon.

Print answer here
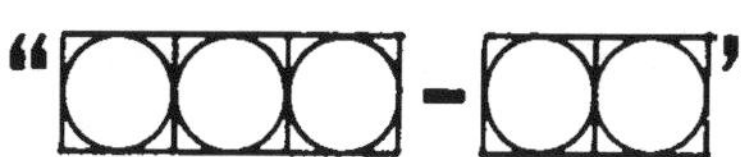

1972
PUZZLE
140

JUMBLE®

Unscramble these four Jumbles, one letter to each square, to form four ordinary words.

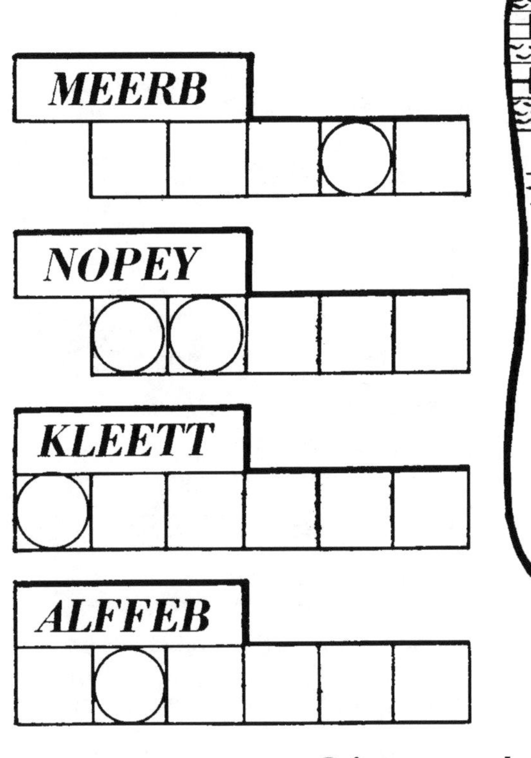
MEERB
NOPEY
KLEETT
ALFFEB

PET SHOP
SOUNDS LIKE YOU MIGHT TAKE A LOOK AT THIS DOG IN CHINA.

Now arrange the circled letters to form the surprise answer, as suggested by the above cartoon.

Print answer here

1972
PUZZLE
141

JUMBLE®

Unscramble these four Jumbles, one letter to each square, to form four ordinary words.

SAYES
RYSAC
DUSHOL
MILDIP
Break it up!
DIVIDES BY UNITING AND UNITES BY DIVIDING.
Print answer here

Now arrange the circled letters to form the surprise answer, as suggested by the above cartoon.

1972
PUZZLE
142

JUMBLE

Unscramble these four Jumbles, one letter to each square, to form four ordinary words.

CADUL

TIFFY

MACENE

DIONIE

NOT TO BE PLAYED WITH WHEN LOADED.

Now arrange the circled letters to form the surprise answer, as suggested by the above cartoon.

Print answer here 

1972
PUZZLE
143

JUMBLE®

Unscramble these four Jumbles, one letter to each square, to form four ordinary words.

KLEAY

SIPOE

THALEC

CHYPIS

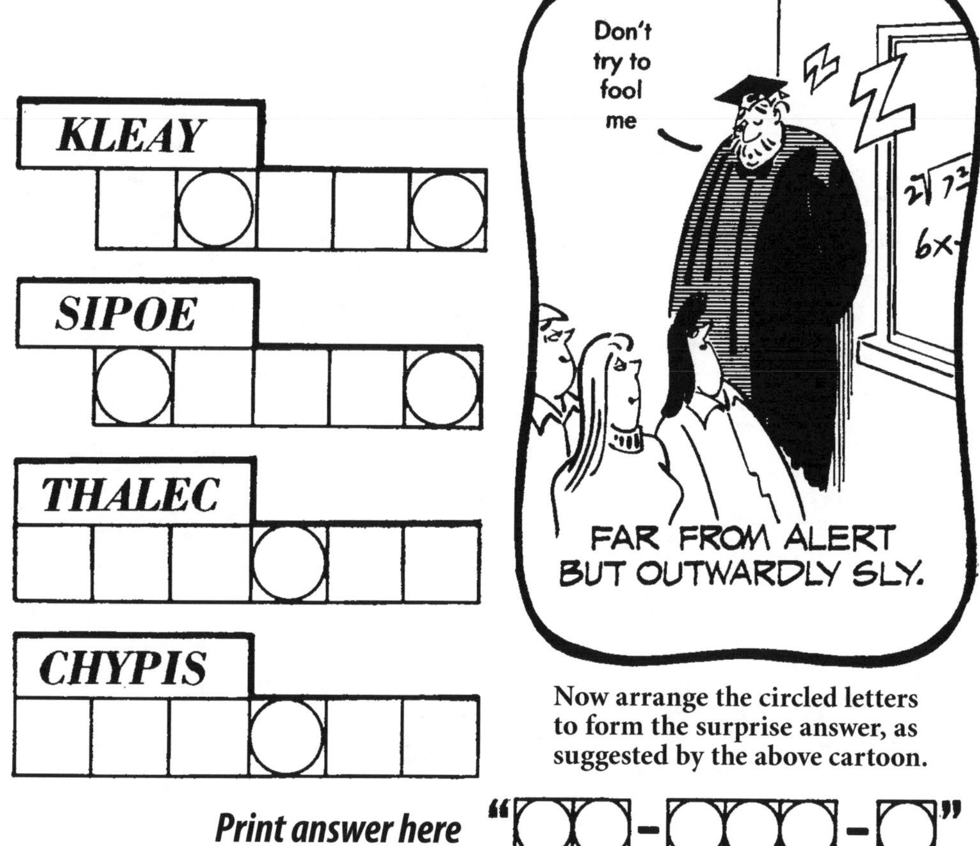
Don't try to fool me
FAR FROM ALERT BUT OUTWARDLY SLY.

Now arrange the circled letters to form the surprise answer, as suggested by the above cartoon.

Print answer here "◯◯-◯◯◯-◯"

1972
PUZZLE
144

JUMBLE®

Unscramble these four Jumbles, one letter to each square, to form four ordinary words.

PREKO

CAIBS

LURCUN

SPOCER

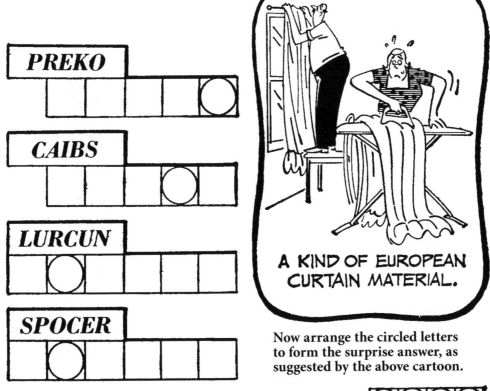

A KIND OF EUROPEAN CURTAIN MATERIAL.

Now arrange the circled letters to form the surprise answer, as suggested by the above cartoon.

Print answer here

1972
PUZZLE
145

JUMBLE®

Unscramble these four Jumbles, one letter to each square, to form four ordinary words.

NOKTE

SKUYH

TIBBEG

GOFTER

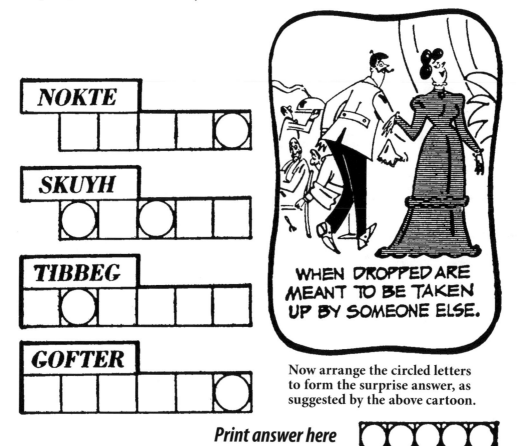

WHEN DROPPED ARE MEANT TO BE TAKEN UP BY SOMEONE ELSE.

Now arrange the circled letters to form the surprise answer, as suggested by the above cartoon.

Print answer here

1972
PUZZLE
146

JUMBLE®

Unscramble these four Jumbles, one letter to each square, to form four ordinary words.

GEWED

CITOX

LEMPOC

PANOWE

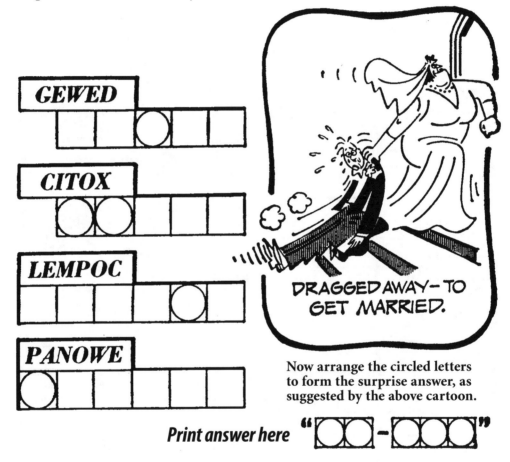

DRAGGED AWAY—TO GET MARRIED.

Now arrange the circled letters to form the surprise answer, as suggested by the above cartoon.

Print answer here "[ ][ ]-[ ][ ][ ]"

1972
PUZZLE
147

JUMBLE®

Unscramble these four Jumbles, one letter to each square, to form four ordinary words.

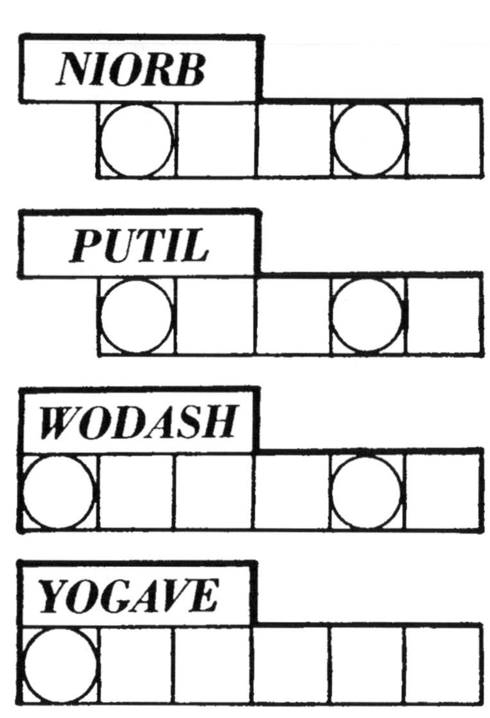
NIORB
PUTIL
WODASH
YOGAVE

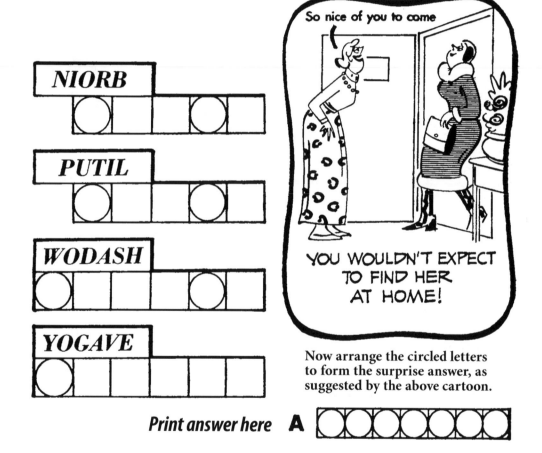

So nice of you to come
YOU WOULDN'T EXPECT TO FIND HER AT HOME!

Now arrange the circled letters to form the surprise answer, as suggested by the above cartoon.

Print answer here A 

1972
PUZZLE
148

JUMBLE®

Unscramble these four Jumbles, one letter to each square, to form four ordinary words.

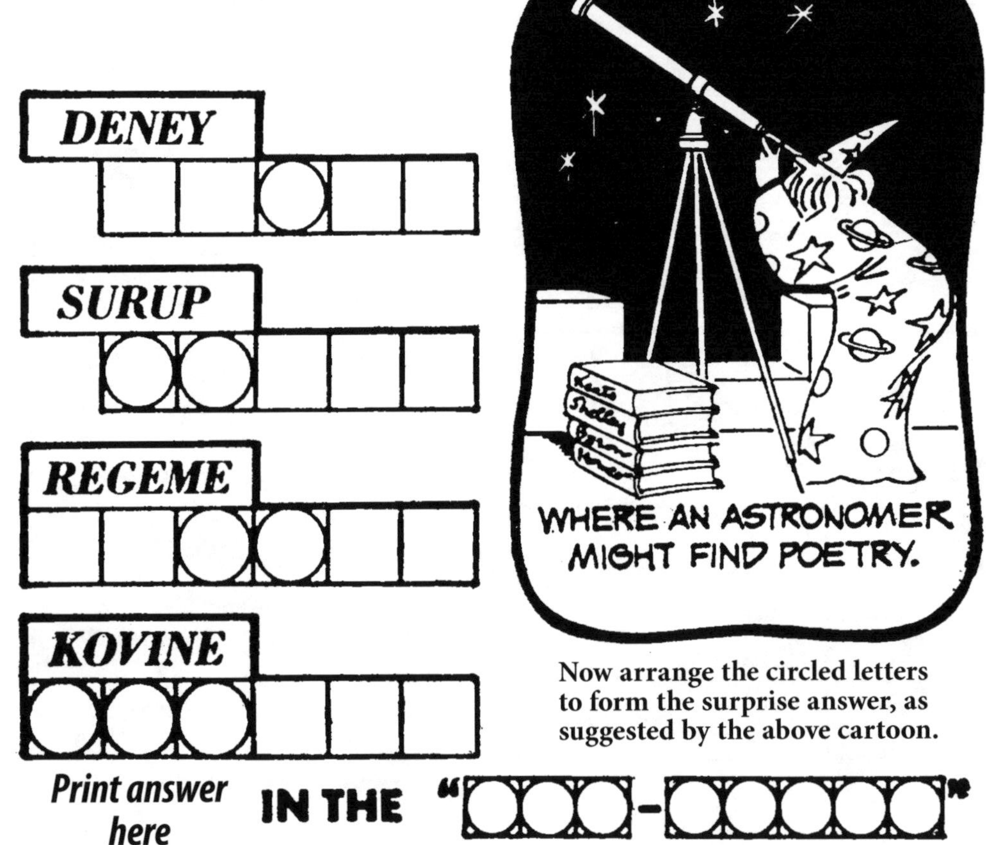

DENEY
SURUP
REGEME
KOVINE
WHERE AN ASTRONOMER MIGHT FIND POETRY.
Print answer here
IN THE "___-______"

Now arrange the circled letters to form the surprise answer, as suggested by the above cartoon.

1972
PUZZLE
149

JUMBLE®

Unscramble these four Jumbles, one letter to each square, to form four ordinary words.

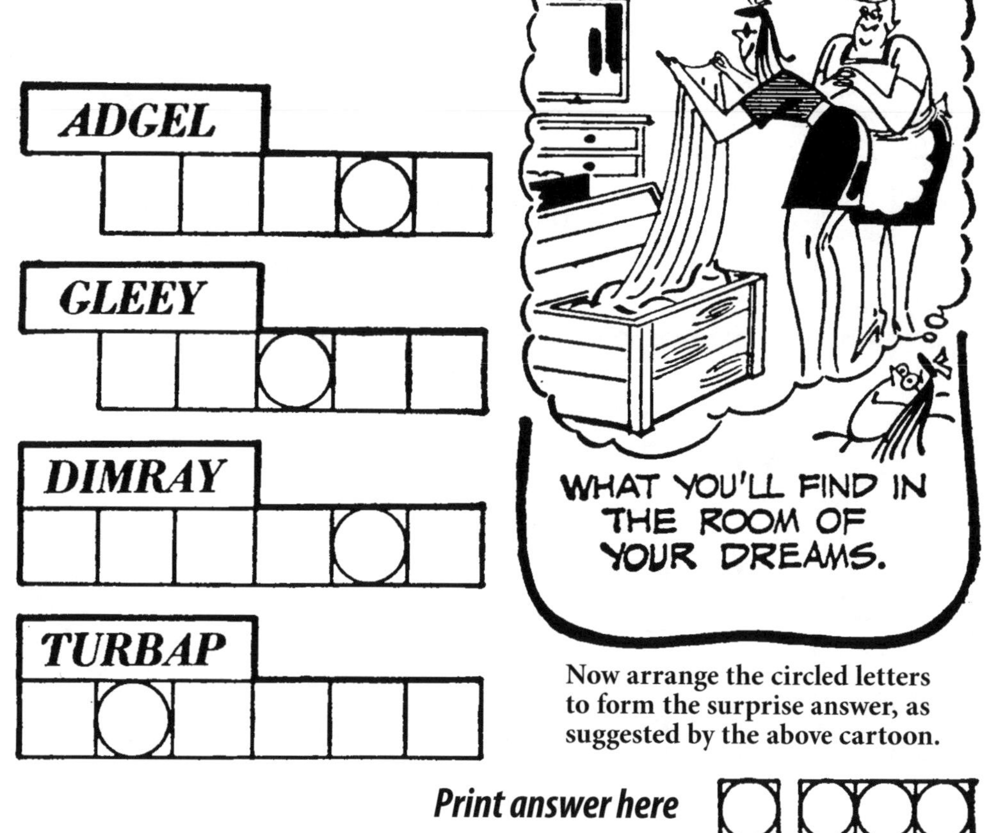
ADGEL
GLEEY
DIMRAY
TURBAP
WHAT YOU'LL FIND IN THE ROOM OF YOUR DREAMS.

Now arrange the circled letters to form the surprise answer, as suggested by the above cartoon.

Print answer here

1972
PUZZLE
150

JUMBLE®

Unscramble these four Jumbles, one letter to each square, to form four ordinary words.

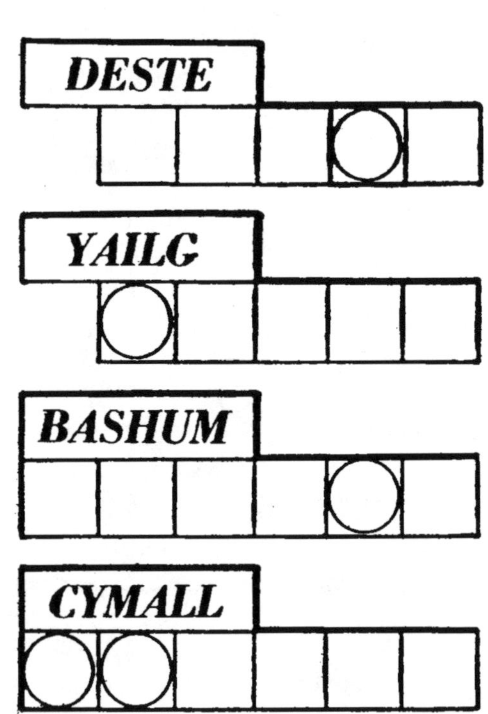
DESTE
YAILG
BASHUM
CYMALL

Cover up!
ZOO
NO SUN-BATHING

MIGHT BE BARRED IN SOME PARKS.

Now arrange the circled letters to form the surprise answer, as suggested by the above cartoon.

Print answer here 

JUMBLE®

Unscramble these four Jumbles, one letter to each square, to form four ordinary words.

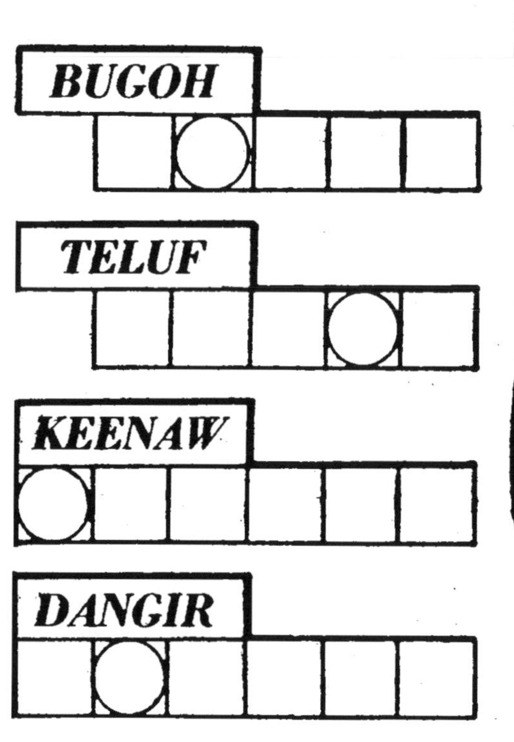
BUGOH
TELUF
KEENAW
DANGIR

Tsk! Tsk! Dead battery!
YOU MIGHT BE POWERLESS TO ACCEPT THIS.

Now arrange the circled letters to form the surprise answer, as suggested by the above cartoon.

Print answer here 

1972
PUZZLE
152

JUMBLE®

Unscramble these four Jumbles, one letter to each square, to form four ordinary words.

TEYIP

DITAU

MERMAH

TAMLED

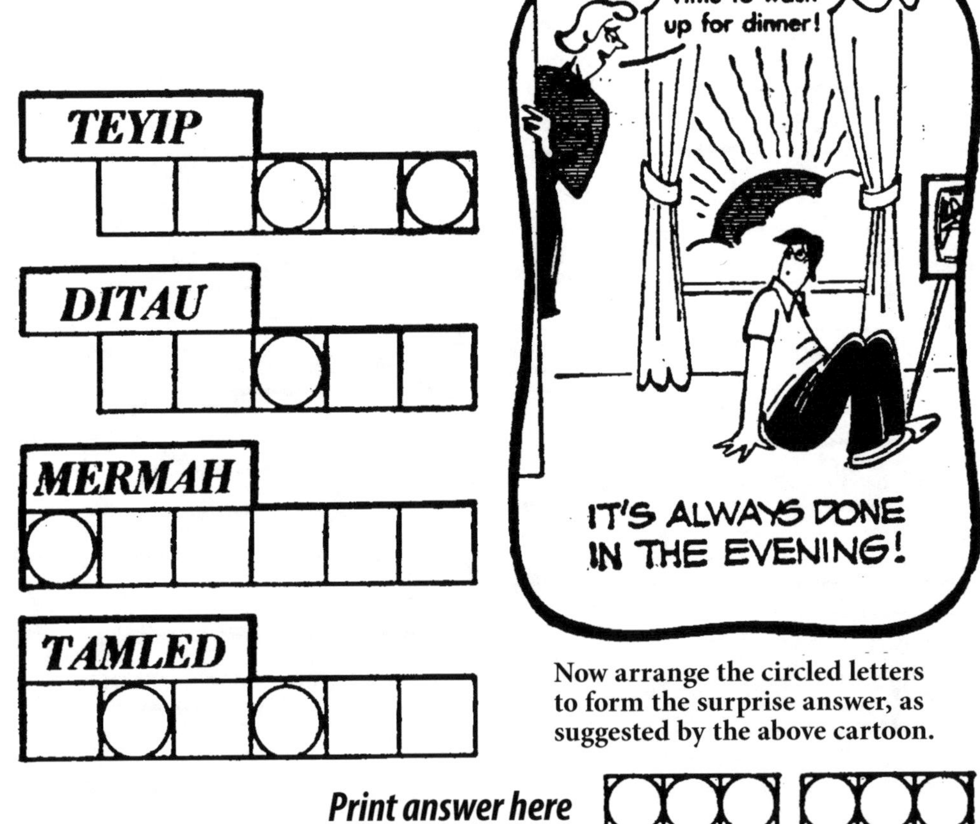

Time to wash up for dinner!
IT'S ALWAYS DONE IN THE EVENING!

Now arrange the circled letters to form the surprise answer, as suggested by the above cartoon.

Print answer here

1972
PUZZLE
153

JUMBLE®

Unscramble these four Jumbles, one letter to each square, to form four ordinary words.

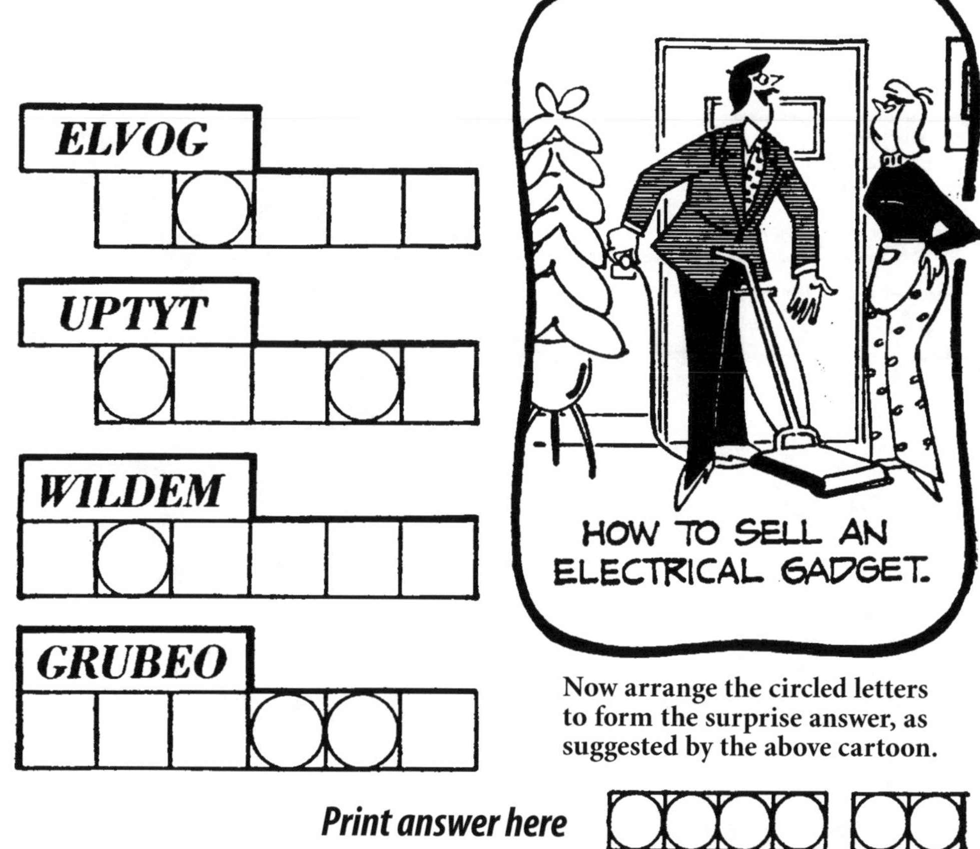
ELVOG
UPTYT
WILDEM
GRUBEO
HOW TO SELL AN ELECTRICAL GADGET.

Now arrange the circled letters to form the surprise answer, as suggested by the above cartoon.

Print answer here

1972
PUZZLE
154

JUMBLE®

Unscramble these four Jumbles, one letter to each square, to form four ordinary words.

INYAR

HALET

CALVEE

FLAUDE

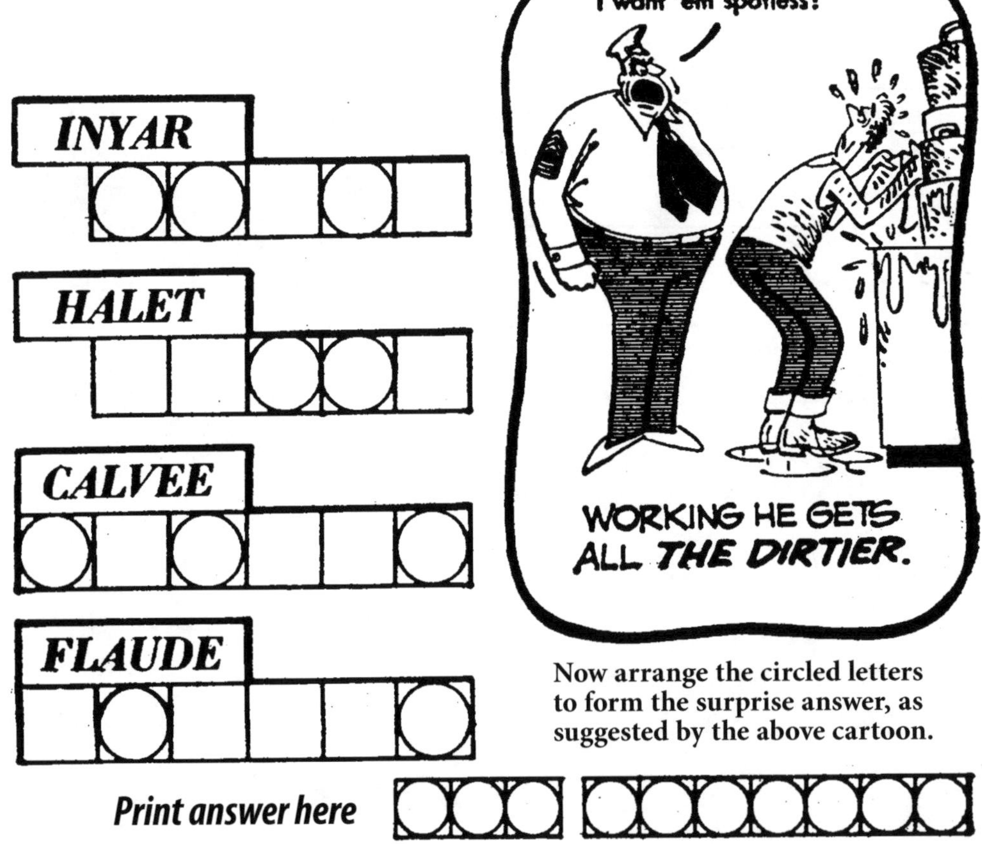
I want 'em spotless!
WORKING HE GETS ALL *THE DIRTIER*.

Now arrange the circled letters to form the surprise answer, as suggested by the above cartoon.

Print answer here

1972 PUZZLE

155

JUMBLE®

Unscramble these four Jumbles, one letter to each square, to form four ordinary words.

CANTE

YADEC

CABEEM

RATTEP

RESTAURANT

LIVERY ENTRANCE

TAKEN DOWN INSIDE.

Now arrange the circled letters to form the surprise answer, as suggested by the above cartoon.

Print answer here

1972 PUZZLE 156

JUMBLE®

Unscramble these four Jumbles, one letter to each square, to form four ordinary words.

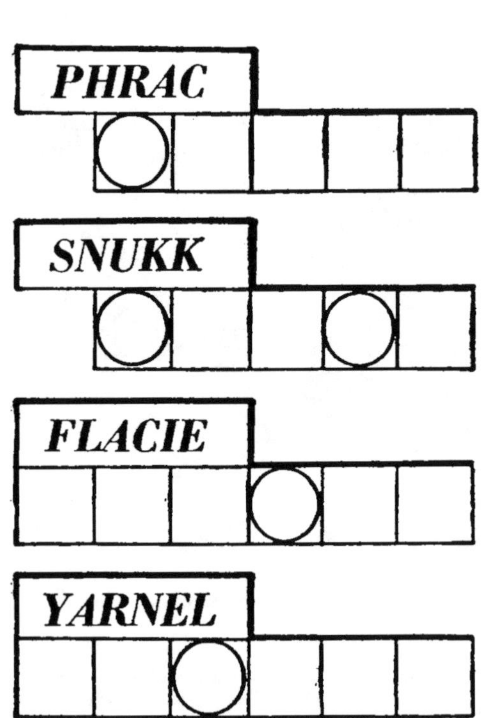

PHRAC
SNUKK
FLACIE
YARNEL

Nice guy—just moved in
WHAT THAT PORTUGUESE NEIGHBOR IS.

Now arrange the circled letters to form the surprise answer, as suggested by the above cartoon.

Print answer here 

1972
PUZZLE
157

JUMBLE®

Unscramble these four Jumbles, one letter to each square, to form four ordinary words.

SIBAN
CAXTE
DESAUB
ANCIDD
"Tomorrow's assignment takes us down to other worlds"
LITERATURE 101
MADE A DENT IN THE HISTORY OF LITERATURE.

Now arrange the circled letters to form the surprise answer, as suggested by the above cartoon.

Print answer here

1972
PUZZLE
158

JUMBLE®

Unscramble these four Jumbles, one letter to each square, to form four ordinary words.

NAGIT

LYDIO

DILBOE

TYKONT

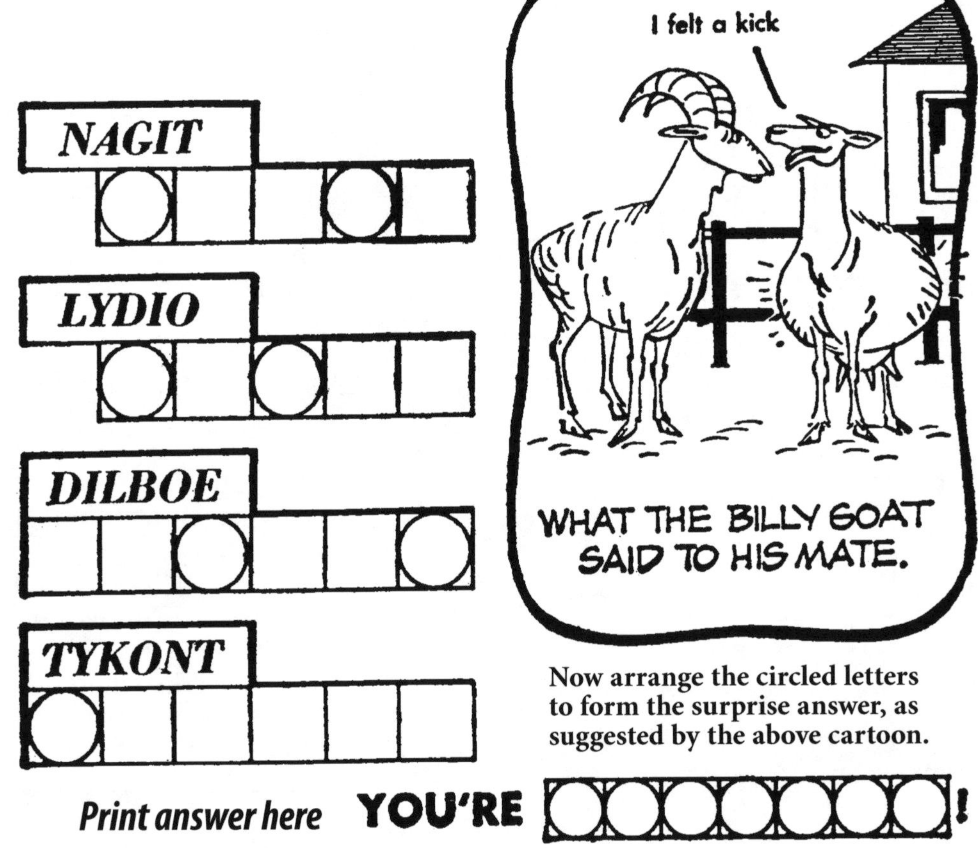
I felt a kick
WHAT THE BILLY GOAT SAID TO HIS MATE.

Now arrange the circled letters to form the surprise answer, as suggested by the above cartoon.

Print answer here **YOU'RE** ________ !

1972 PUZZLE

159

JUMBLE®

Unscramble these four Jumbles, one letter to each square, to form four ordinary words.

TENFO

ITUSE

RUGLAF

YORTHE

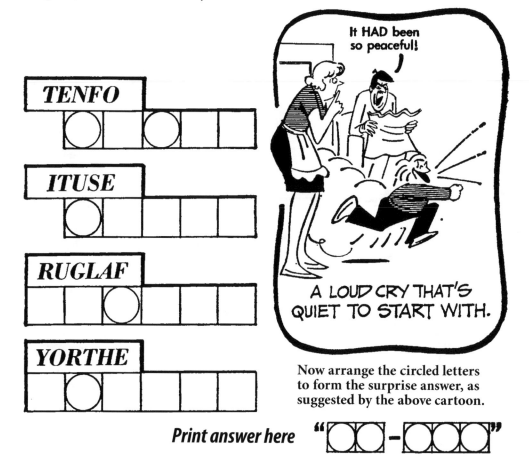

It HAD been so peaceful!

A LOUD CRY THAT'S QUIET TO START WITH.

Now arrange the circled letters to form the surprise answer, as suggested by the above cartoon.

Print answer here "[ ][ ]-[ ][ ][ ]"

1972
PUZZLE
160

JUMBLE®

Unscramble these four Jumbles, one letter to each square, to form four ordinary words.

WOPOH

UNEES

TADEEB

ENMURB

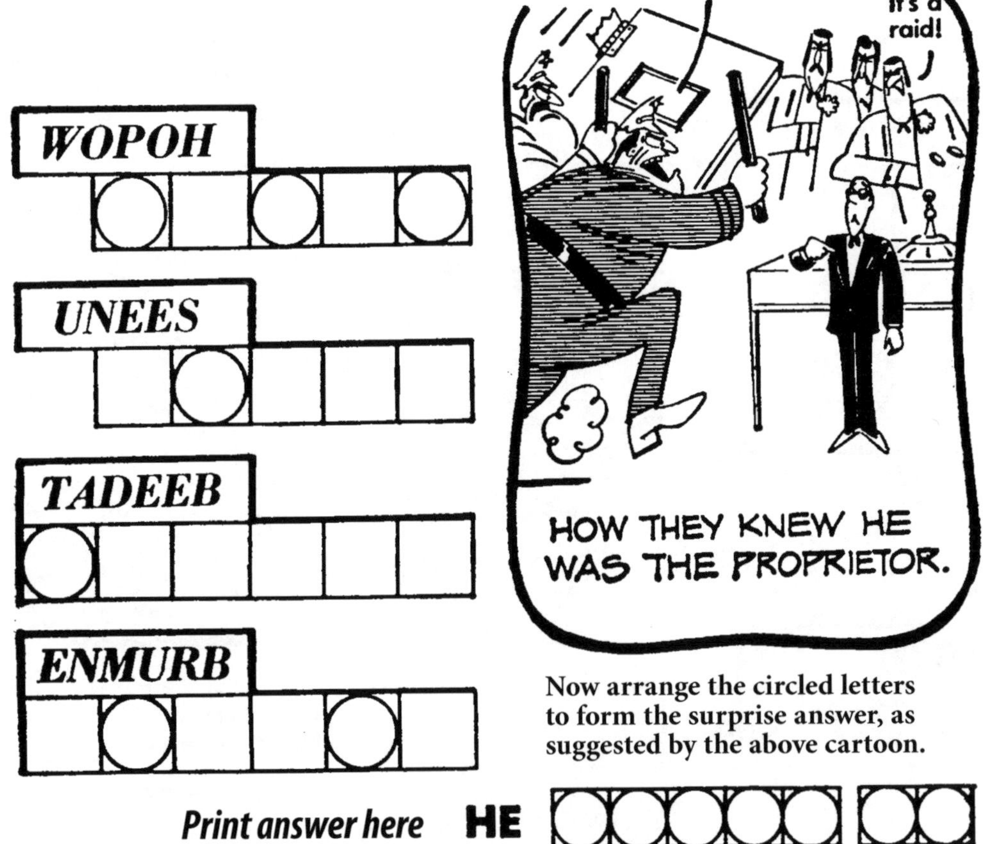

Who's the big boss here?
It's a raid!
HOW THEY KNEW HE WAS THE PROPRIETOR.

Now arrange the circled letters to form the surprise answer, as suggested by the above cartoon.

Print answer here **HE**

JUMBLE

TIME MACHINE: 1972

Challenger Puzzles

1972
PUZZLE
161

JUMBLE®

Unscramble these six Jumbles, one letter to each square, to form six ordinary words.

DIPALL

CINTAG

HERTIE

COALJE

DEFUNC

OKOCIE

HEE HO
HOO HOO

WHY HE DIED LAUGHING.

Now arrange the circled letters to form the surprise answer, as suggested by the above cartoon.

Print answer here HE WAS ________ TO ______

JUMBLE®

Unscramble these six Jumbles, one letter to each square, to form six ordinary words.

TANCAV

GWEEDD

LEMOTE

THERTE

YAIRFT

MANNEP

No discount?
YOUR FARE SHOULD BE REDUCED IF YOU'RE THIS.

Now arrange the circled letters to form the surprise answer, as suggested by the above cartoon.

Print answer here

1972 PUZZLE

163

JUMBLE®

Unscramble these six Jumbles, one letter to each square, to form six ordinary words.

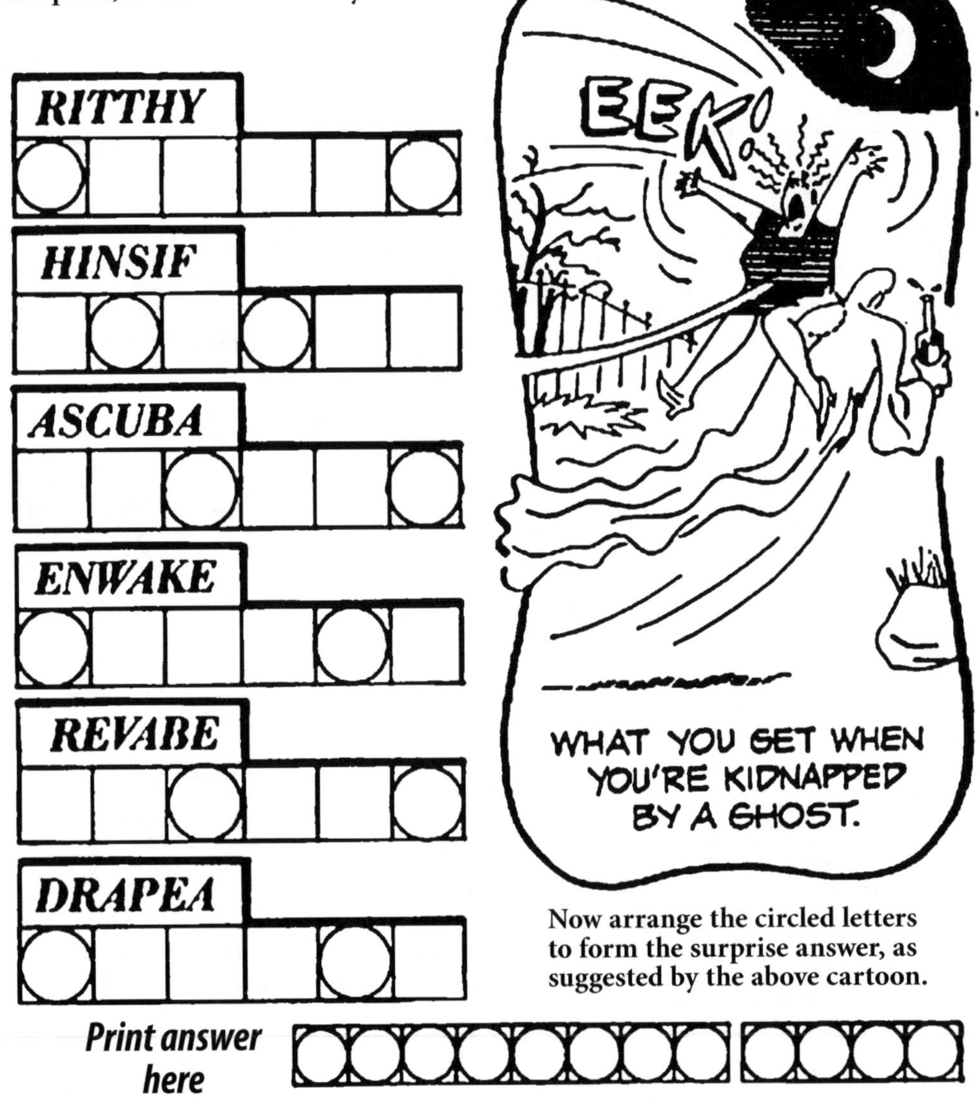

RITTHY
HINSIF
ASCUBA
ENWAKE
REVABE
DRAPEA
EEK!
WHAT YOU GET WHEN YOU'RE KIDNAPPED BY A GHOST.
Now arrange the circled letters to form the surprise answer, as suggested by the above cartoon.
Print answer here

1972
PUZZLE
164

JUMBLE®
Unscramble these six Jumbles, one letter to each square, to form six ordinary words.
VYCOON
FESTOF
USDABE
VERDIF
NUIRJY
BIGTLE
Why is she marrying an officer?
Now arrange the circled letters to form the surprise answer, as suggested by the above cartoon.

Print answer here

"HE MADE A ▢▢▢▢▢ ▢▢▢▢▢▢, ▢▢▢!"

1972
PUZZLE
165

JUMBLE®

Unscramble these six Jumbles, one letter to each square, to form six ordinary words.

DUMEGS

HIALAD

CANTIO

OTTYNK

GRUFIE

PYRSOD

MAKE MUSIC—
AND NONSENSE!

Now arrange the circled letters to form the surprise answer, as suggested by the above cartoon.

Print answer here !

1972
PUZZLE
166

JUMBLE®

Unscramble these six Jumbles, one letter to each square, to form six ordinary words.

SACCUT
MAHREM
COBORN
BOYDEM
THANYS
PREEWT
He can't run!
HORSE DOCTOR
WHY THE JOCKEY CALLED THE VET.
Now arrange the circled letters to form the surprise answer, as suggested by the above cartoon.
Print answer here
HIS
WAS

1972
PUZZLE
167

JUMBLE®

Unscramble these six Jumbles, one letter to each square, to form six ordinary words.

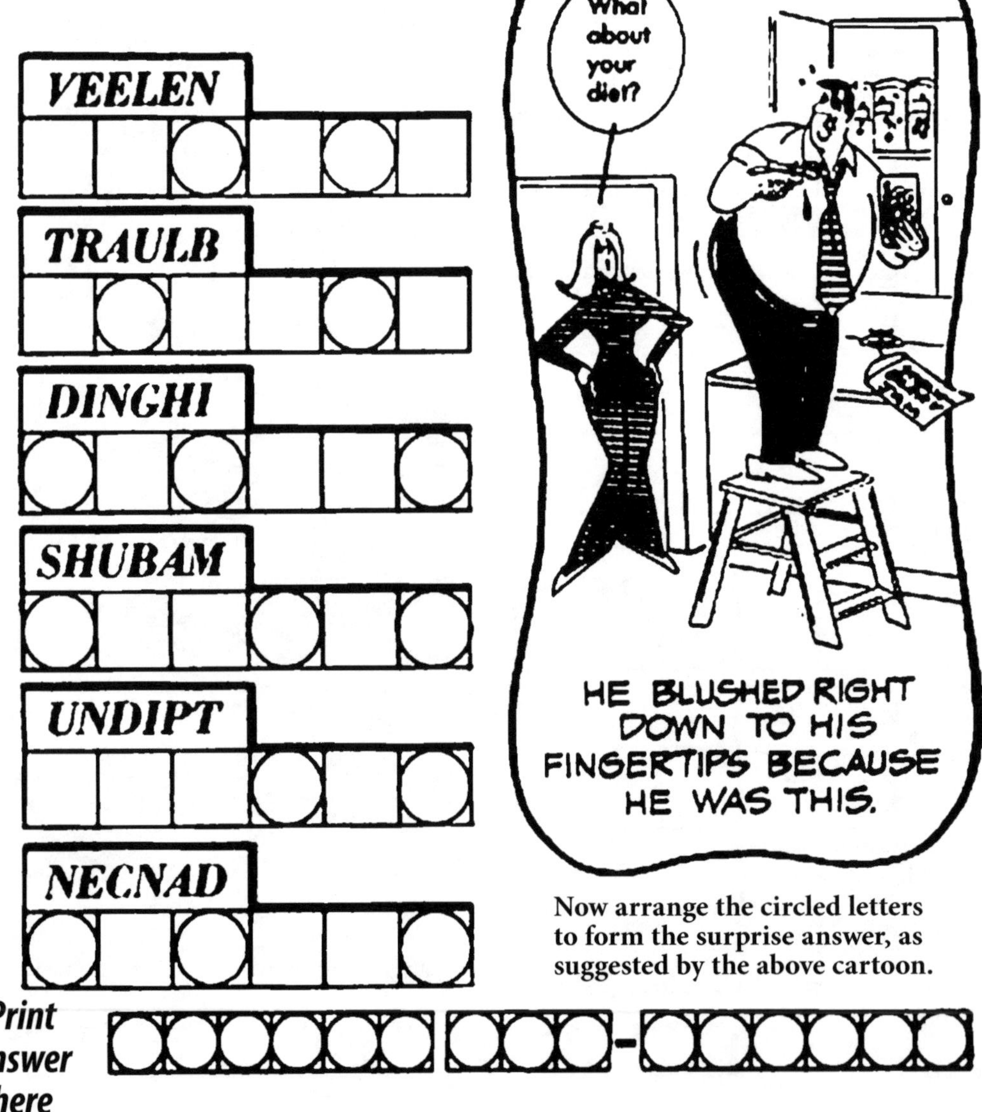
VEELEN
TRAULB
DINGHI
SHUBAM
UNDIPT
NECNAD
What about your diet?
HE BLUSHED RIGHT DOWN TO HIS FINGERTIPS BECAUSE HE WAS THIS.
Now arrange the circled letters to form the surprise answer, as suggested by the above cartoon.
Print answer here

1972 PUZZLE

168

JUMBLE®

Unscramble these six Jumbles, one letter to each square, to form six ordinary words.

MARKEB
NOALOS
EXDOUT
DRIHNE
GLACEY
CHISPY
WHAT HE WAS WHEN HE FOUND A PEARL IN THE OYSTER.

Now arrange the circled letters to form the surprise answer, as suggested by the above cartoon.

Print answer here “ ”

1972 PUZZLE

169

JUMBLE®

Unscramble these six Jumbles, one letter to each square, to form six ordinary words.

YEKTUR

MUCAUV

GLOIBE

PUMITE

YASUNE

DOSTIL

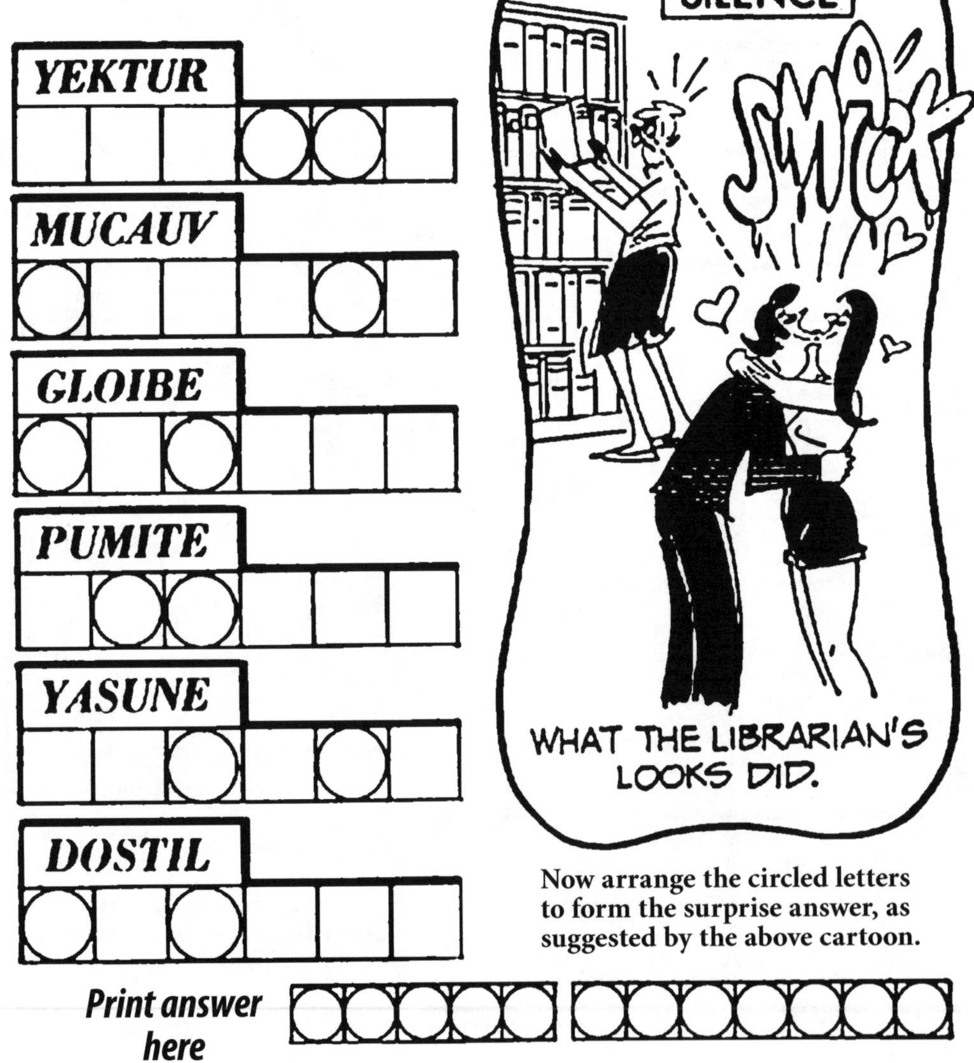
SILENCE
SMACK
WHAT THE LIBRARIAN'S LOOKS DID.

Now arrange the circled letters to form the surprise answer, as suggested by the above cartoon.

Print answer here

1972 PUZZLE

170

JUMBLE®

Unscramble these six Jumbles, one letter to each square, to form six ordinary words.

TULNAW
CUBDAT
MAIROH
NATQUI
LAGYAX
ROLARP
He won't pay
Take him in
TAXI
YOU'LL BE CHARGED AFTER A RIDE IN THIS.

Now arrange the circled letters to form the surprise answer, as suggested by the above cartoon.

Print answer here **A**

1972
PUZZLE
171

JUMBLE®

Unscramble these six Jumbles, one letter to each square, to form six ordinary words.

YARVOS

GINDAR

BETASK

MIDYOF

VINTAY

LESUNS

On the house
On the house
On the house
HOW MUCH CAN A FREELOADER DRINK?

Now arrange the circled letters to form the surprise answer, as suggested by the above cartoon.

Print answer here

JUMBLE®

Unscramble these six Jumbles, one letter to each square, to form six ordinary words.

ENMUIM

BEEDAT

PARTTE

HOMAFT

RARQUY

BOUTES

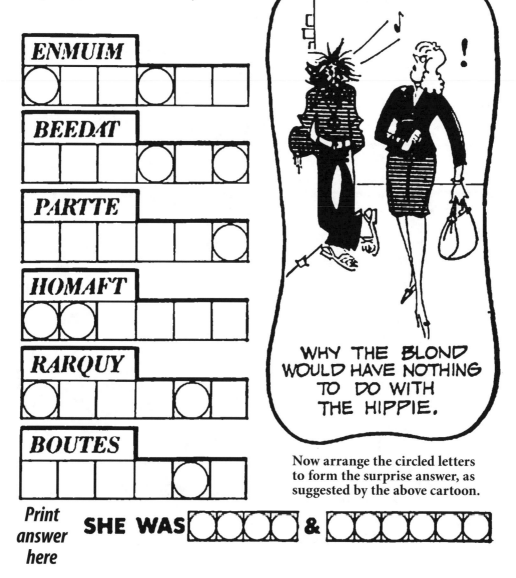

WHY THE BLOND WOULD HAVE NOTHING TO DO WITH THE HIPPIE.

Now arrange the circled letters to form the surprise answer, as suggested by the above cartoon.

Print answer here SHE WAS ☐☐☐☐☐ & ☐☐☐☐☐☐☐

1972
PUZZLE
173

JUMBLE®

Unscramble these six Jumbles, one letter to each square, to form six ordinary words.

STEGAK

TINSEV

VAHILS

CYGERL

TAUMER

CAIFLE

EEK!!
WHY IS A MOUSE LIKE GRASS?

Now arrange the circled letters to form the surprise answer, as suggested by the above cartoon.

Print answer here THE ___’ __ ___ __

1972
PUZZLE
174

JUMBLE®

Unscramble these six Jumbles, one letter to each square, to form six ordinary words.

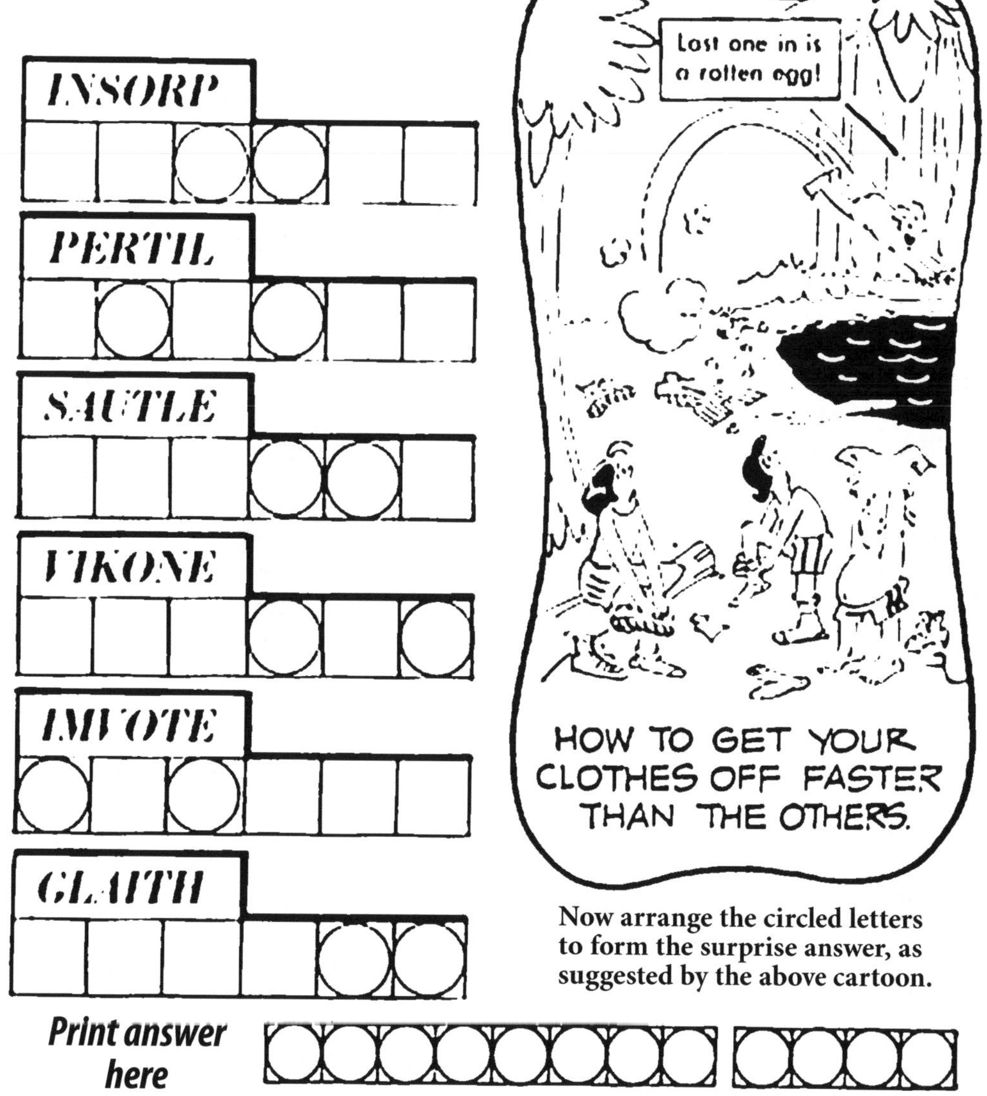
INSORP
PERTIL
SAUTLE
VIKONE
IMVOTE
GLAITH
Lost one in is a rotten egg!
HOW TO GET YOUR CLOTHES OFF FASTER THAN THE OTHERS.
Print answer here

Now arrange the circled letters to form the surprise answer, as suggested by the above cartoon.

1972
PUZZLE
175

JUMBLE®

Unscramble these six Jumbles, one letter to each square, to form six ordinary words.

FASTIE

UNGOTE

REEBOF

YEMITS

CYTHAC

TELPOI

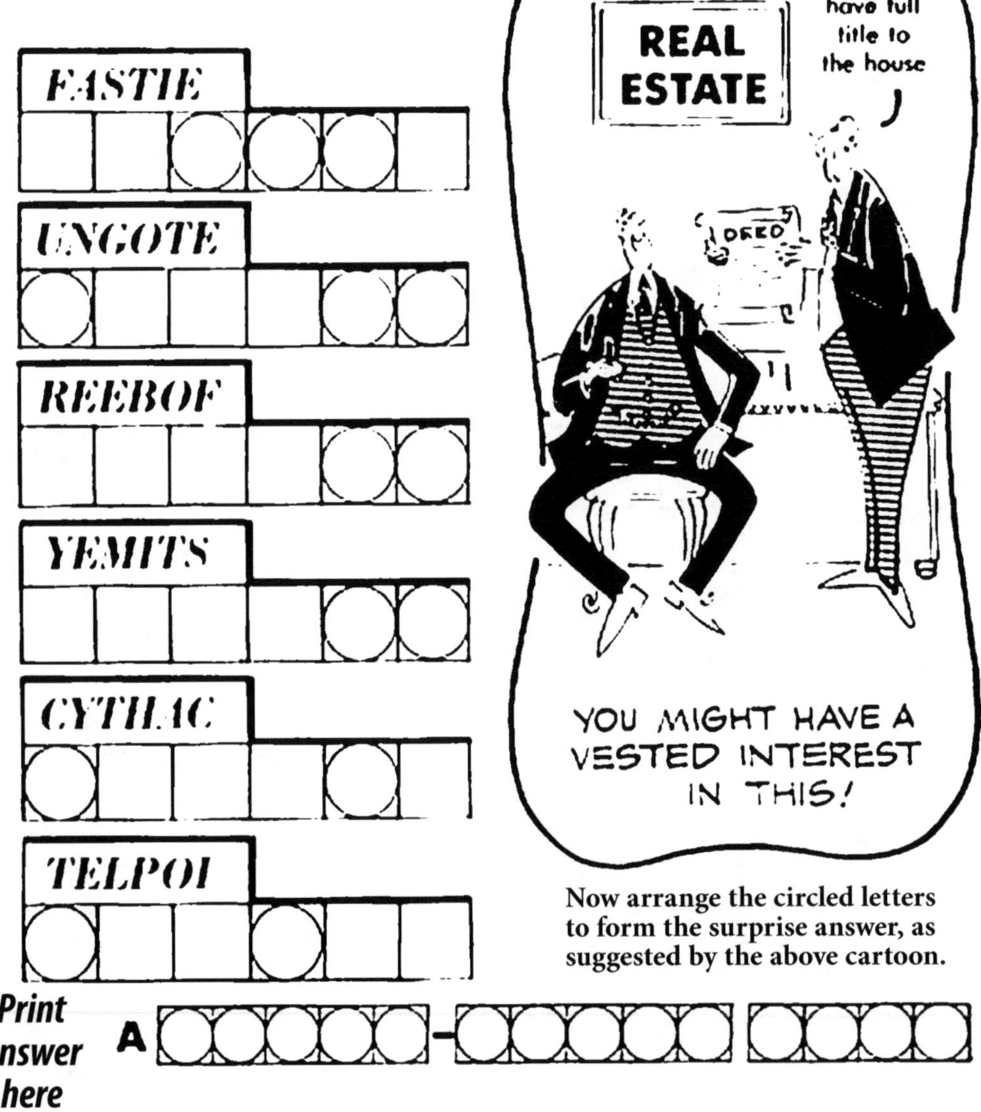
REAL
ESTATE
You now have full title to the house
DEED
YOU MIGHT HAVE A VESTED INTEREST IN THIS!

Now arrange the circled letters to form the surprise answer, as suggested by the above cartoon.

Print answer here A [ ]-[ ] [ ]

JUMBLE®

Unscramble these six Jumbles, one letter to each square, to form six ordinary words.

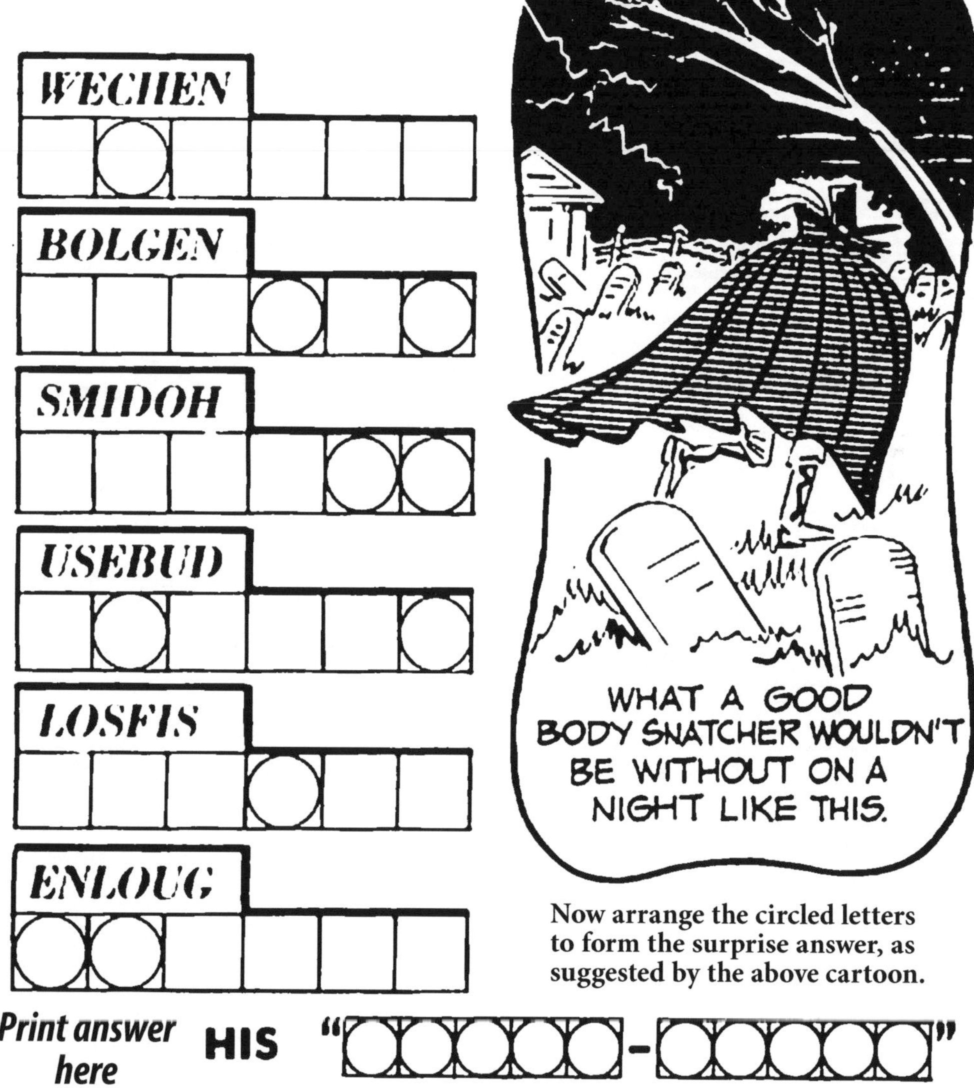
WECHEN
BOLGEN
SMIDOH
USEBUD
LOSFIS
ENLOUG
WHAT A GOOD BODY SNATCHER WOULDN'T BE WITHOUT ON A NIGHT LIKE THIS.

Now arrange the circled letters to form the surprise answer, as suggested by the above cartoon.

Print answer here HIS "[ ][ ][ ][ ][ ]-[ ][ ][ ][ ][ ]"

1972
PUZZLE
177

JUMBLE®

Unscramble these six Jumbles, one letter to each square, to form six ordinary words.

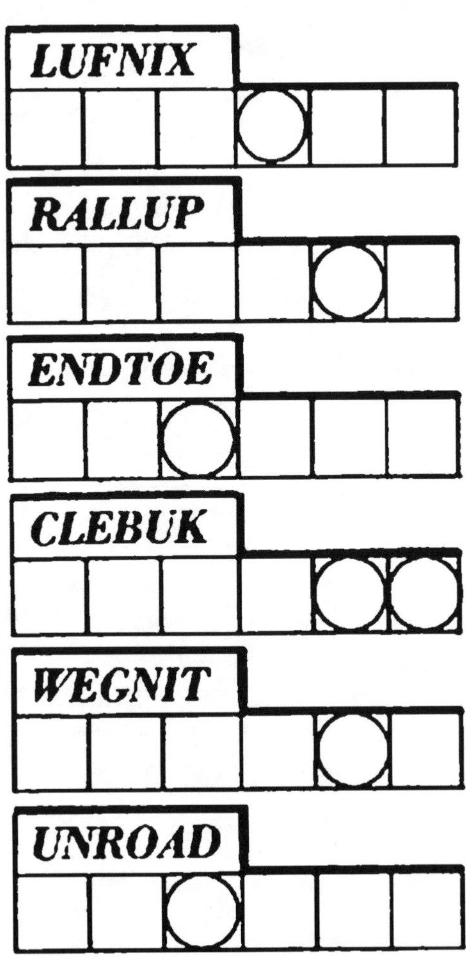
LUFNIX
RALLUP
ENDTOE
CLEBUK
WEGNIT
UNROAD

XXX
THIS VESSEL CONTAINS JUST A LITTLE MORE THAN FOUR QUARTS.

Now arrange the circled letters to form the surprise answer, as suggested by the above cartoon.

Print answer here **A "◯◯◯◯-◯-◯◯"**

1972
PUZZLE
178

JUMBLE®

Unscramble these six Jumbles, one letter to each square, to form six ordinary words.

TRAWEY
FELBAF
YORCAN
GEOVAY
DEMANT
ENGINS
I refuse to answer on the grounds . . . (yak yak yak)
He doesn't say much but he has a tough reputation
WHAT YOU WOULDN'T EXPECT TO GET FROM A MAN OF FEW WORDS.

Now arrange the circled letters to form the surprise answer, as suggested by the above cartoon.

Print answer here A

1972
PUZZLE
179

JUMBLE®

Unscramble these six Jumbles, one letter to each square, to form six ordinary words.

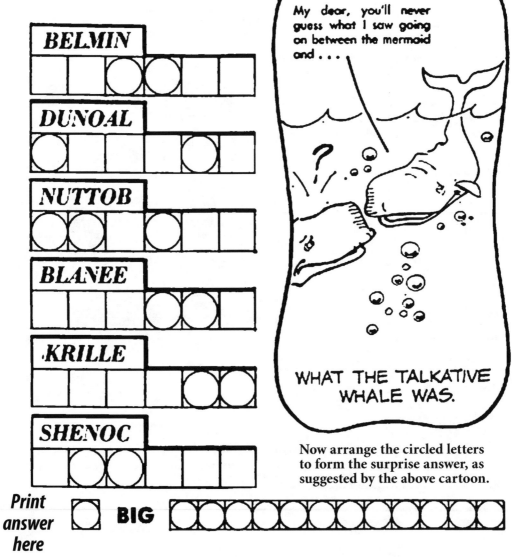

BELMIN

		◯	◯		

DUNOAL

◯				◯	

NUTTOB

◯	◯		◯		

BLANEE

			◯	◯	

KRILLE

				◯	◯

SHENOC

	◯	◯			

My dear, you'll never guess what I saw going on between the mermaid and . . .

WHAT THE TALKATIVE WHALE WAS.

Now arrange the circled letters to form the surprise answer, as suggested by the above cartoon.

Print answer here ◯ **BIG** ◯◯◯◯◯◯◯◯◯◯◯◯

1972 PUZZLE

180

JUMBLE®

Unscramble these six Jumbles, one letter to each square, to form six ordinary words.

JINNOE
ROPPEH
SMARDI
LOUBES
GIZZAG
YINTTE
So long
Last drinks
AT A PLACE LIKE THIS EXPECT THEM AT CLOSING TIME.

Now arrange the circled letters to form the surprise answer, as suggested by the above cartoon.

Print answer here

Answers

1. **Jumbles:** GOOSE PHONY FROSTY BOTANY
Answer: Odd if they're both right!—SHOES

2. **Jumbles:** PIVOT FORUM DENTAL MIDDAY
Answer: It's the same in many countries—"DITTO"

3. **Jumbles:** RODEO PIANO BICEPS ERMINE
Answer: Gets paid after his work is finished—A PENSIONER

4. **Jumbles:** POUND CROUP ASYLUM SIPHON
Answer: This is neither very good nor very bad—so, repeat it!—SO-SO

5. **Jumbles:** PHOTO DAILY BOTTLE FLORID
Answer: Why the gunman and his gun were dangerous—BOTH WERE LOADED

6. **Jumbles:** WHOSE PARTY NOVICE CANINE
Answer: This might be responsible for a certain coolness at the top—A SNOWCAP

7. **Jumbles:** NUDGE ANNOY URCHIN BRIDLE
Answer: What the frustrated racehorse was always getting—THE RUNAROUND

8. **Jumbles:** DRAMA LINGO MODERN CELERY
Answer: You have to have grounds to be this—A LANDLORD

9. **Jumbles:** CHAIR PATIO FAMOUS MANAGE
Answer: Twice a mother—MAMA

10. **Jumbles:** DEPOT ANKLE MORBID PLAGUE
Answer: Late in bed and delayed—"BE-LATE-D"

11. **Jumbles:** WHILE DOGMA PICNIC BROOCH
Answer: Why she married the artist—SHE WAS DRAWN TO HIM

12. **Jumbles:** TAFFY OLDER PAUNCH BLAZER
Answer: This is the result of a musical strike—A NOTE

13. **Jumbles:** VAGUE TRILL FAULTY BODICE
Answer: This would indicate that someone has just stopped smoking—A LIVE BUTT

14. **Jumbles:** ANNUL SCOUT GRATIS MIDWAY
Answer: It's more usual to have only half of this—TWINS

15. **Jumbles:** FORCE ARBOR MARROW PLEDGE
Answer: Might be mad about the engine—"LOCO"

16. **Jumbles:** IRONY SAUTE PEPSIN FARINA
Answer: Goes off to report trouble—A SIREN

17. **Jumbles:** LURID SWAMP MARVEL CALIPH
Answer: Completely tied up in postal regulations!—PARCELS

18. **Jumbles:** LYRIC FAVOR BUTANE MEDLEY
Answer: How the fat man spoke—BROADLY

19. **Jumbles:** INEPT WEARY UNTRUE CIPHER
Answer: Unusual to have a warm relationship with this—WINTER

20. **Jumbles:** EIGHT ABIDE METRIC BANANA
Answer: What happens when you encourage a gambler—YOU "A-BET" HIM

21. **Jumbles:** OUNCE FUROR PAYOFF DEFACE
Answer: This street meeting might give you a turn!—A CORNER

22. **Jumbles:** DEITY ABYSS BEHELD PUSHER
Answer: At the bottom of successful gardening—SEEDS

23. **Jumbles:** MOSSY CHANT OPPOSE GLOOMY
Answer: Pals broken up in the mountains—ALPS

24. **Jumbles:** LINEN VISTA POETRY CONVEX
Answer: Your financial problems melt away when you're this!—SOLVENT

25. **Jumbles:** AHEAD SWOON TRICKY GIGGLE
Answer: How good models are built—TO SCALE

26. **Jumbles:** NAVAL GIVEN DEPUTY GLOBAL
Answer: Sometimes goes around to provide comfort—A BANDAGE

27. **Jumbles:** GUILT DEMON VERBAL PIRACY
Answer: How the road gang entertained the drivers—BY DIVERTING THEM

28. **Jumbles:** UNITY HIKER OSSIFY ARTFUL
Answer: Provides marriage guidance—AN USHER

29. **Jumbles:** DERBY PLAID SLEIGH FACADE
Answer: What the tattoo artist turned gunman drew on his victims—BEADS

30. **Jumbles:** LAUGH PYLON RELISH FLAUNT
Answer: How a miser practices philanthropy—SPARINGLY

31. **Jumbles:** EVENT CHOIR LETHAL HECTIC
Answer: This shows promise—A CONTRACT

32. **Jumbles:** PIKER GUEST MISUSE HUNGRY
Answer: They contract to give you a comfortable ride—SPRINGS

33. **Jumbles:** ADAPT SLANT COUPLE ROSARY
Answer: How to get good looks—STARE

34. **Jumbles:** AGATE FEIGN NOBODY COMMON
Answer: He won't stand for anything!—AN INFANT

35. **Jumbles:** AORTA FAULT ALWAYS JACKAL
Answer: How not to leave a door if you don't want them to steal a vase—"A-JAR"

36. **Jumbles:** LANKY AFIRE CRAVAT FICKLE
Answer: You have to be it with the first letter before you can be it without the first—L-EARNER

37. **Jumbles:** ELITE SNARL OPIATE MORTAR
Answer: Theater performances not open to the public—OPERATIONS

38. **Jumbles:** FAMED ENVOY OCCULT PULPIT
Answer: Sometimes carries poison and sounds awful—"VIAL"

39. **Jumbles:** DOUSE GROIN LAYOFF PRAYER
Answer: What might be hidden in a garden?—DANGER

40. **Jumbles:** PUPIL HOVEL DISCUS QUARTZ
Answer: This would describe a high-spirited chiseler—"CHIPPER"

41. **Jumbles:** DIRTY AGING PLACID VIOLIN
Answer: This is used in summing up—ADDITION

42. **Jumbles:** IRATE VALUE SKEWER BLEACH
Answer: Might be straining to do a job—A SIEVE

43. **Jumbles:** VIGIL WAKEN THRESH LAWYER
Answer: This view may help you get a job—AN INTERVIEW

44. **Jumbles:** DAISY CREEL AROUSE STURDY
Answer: They insure the correct delivery of speeches—ADDRESSES

45. **Jumbles:** AWOKE MINOR CLIENT BONNET
Answer: You just can't shut your eyes to this!—LOOK

46. **Jumbles:** BUXOM INKED CAUCUS FALTER
Answer: This might be composed of mud and air—RADIUM

47. **Jumbles:** ERUPT GAUGE PASTRY INCOME
Answer: They might be carried by cards—GREETINGS

48. **Jumbles:** BEGUN SAVOR GARISH PROFIT
Answer: Today's answer will dawn on you tomorrow—SUNRISE

49. **Jumbles:** PROBE TARDY BALLAD GIBBON
Answer: What he was was apparent—A PARENT

50. **Jumbles:** OPIUM ENJOY REALTY LIZARD
Answer: Once aroused you may lose it!—YOUR TEMPER

51. **Jumbles:** LUSTY FENCE POROUS GRISLY
Answer: From a ruse, you can make certain of this—SURE

52. **Jumbles:** INLET HAVEN THORAX GAMBOL
Answer: As long as you are—it's yours—HEIGHT

53. **Jumbles:** BATHE PAYEE CLOUDY ICEBOX
Answer: Ran down the beach—EBBED

54. **Jumbles:** EPOCH APART BETAKE FLORAL
Answer: Might mean some drip let the secrets out—A "LEAK"

55. **Jumbles:** VERVE TOOTH DEVICE BANNER
Answer: Try and give this to a prisoner—THE VERDICT

56. **Jumbles:** SUAVE HANDY POWDER LIQUID
Answer: What a top hat might make—YOUR HEAD SPIN

57. **Jumbles:** MUSIC TRIPE DAWNED ANEMIA
Answer: What you'd expect from a little devil—"IMP-UDENCE"

58. **Jumbles:** DROOP EXULT BEWARE VOLUME
Answer: This is owing to being late—OVERDUE

59. **Jumbles:** NEWLY BARON POLLEN AUTUMN
Answer: Make nothing of it!—ANNUL

60. **Jumbles:** MAUVE ITCHY FUTURE GRIMLY
Answer: They do like each other—IMITATE

61. **Jumbles:** ACRID DRAFT IMPAIR ENZYME
Answer: What a doctor puts on before he starts working—AN "M D"

62. **Jumbles:** DANDY TWEET BOTHER RITUAL
Answer: How to offer them better meat—"TENDER" IT

63. **Jumbles:** ONION PLAIT HOTBED TOUCHY
Answer: What you think is yours—OPINION

64. **Jumbles:** IGLOO VALOR MALLET ACHING
Answer: Why leaving your old home might be emotionally disturbing—IT'S "MOVING"

65. **Jumbles:** YOUNG FANCY HAPPEN LEVITY
Answer: Make many a slip!—NYLON

66. **Jumbles:** LATCH BELIE SHAKEN MEMOIR
Answer: Might be in the sale at the fur shop—"SA-B-LE"

67. **Jumbles:** VISOR ETUDE AGENCY NATURE
Answer: What they drove back in—REVERSE

68. **Jumbles:** OWING CHOKE SLOGAN IRONIC
Answer: It's definitely a racket!—NOISE

69. **Jumbles:** LOOSE ALIAS MATRON GOSPEL
Answer: Festivity with a gal—A GALA

70. **Jumbles:** ABATE RANCH BIKINI TURNIP
Answer: You wouldn't want to go to the doctor if you suffered from this—INERTIA

71. **Jumbles:** DINER LOVER ABOUND BRANDY
Answer: A puzzling way to make holes—RIDDLE

72. **Jumbles:** NOVEL GRIPE ABSORB DAINTY
Answer: Provides the main course on board ship—THE NAVIGATOR

73. **Jumbles:** MERCY FAITH NICELY GOITER
Answer: Tell this guy to go to blazes—and you'll get a response out of him!—A FIREMAN

74. **Jumbles:** BANJO TYPED HANDLE FASTEN
Answer: They sometimes work around the clock on the farm—"HANDS"

75. **Jumbles:** DAUNT CHAMP SUBMIT INVERT
Answer: Background material for an artist—CANVAS

76. **Jumbles:** TABOO CHEEK BLUISH INDOOR
Answer: If it's still there, there isn't any—ACTION

77. **Jumbles:** BIRCH GLAND OUTCRY RAGLAN
Answer: This is the least you can do!—NOTHING

78. **Jumbles:** COLIC KINKY UNSAID PLAQUE
Answer: "Jump, miss"—SKIP

79. **Jumbles:** SMACK OPERA ASSAIL HOMAGE
Answer: How you might smell the beginning of a romance—WITH AN "A-ROMA"

80. **Jumbles:** DRAWL LOONY JURIST PODIUM
Answer: Made to come clean before the hanging!—LAUNDRY

81. **Jumbles:** GUESS MESSY LEGUME POPLAR
Answer: He declared—he wasn't one!—A SMUGGLER

82. **Jumbles:** NOTCH ERASE PONCHO INVADE
Answer: Oddly enough what this might be!—NOT EVEN

83. **Jumbles:** MOUSE RIVET PRIMER SPLICE
Answer: You wouldn't be prepared to make such a speech!—IMPROMPTU

84. **Jumbles:** BURLY GORGE ACTING CLOTHE
Answer: You can feel this but not get it!—YOUNGER

85. **Jumbles:** MINER SCARF BYWORD DAMPEN
Answer: May be shot in a boat—RAPIDS

86. **Jumbles:** CRAZE BUSHY IMPORT MISHAP
Answer: You might find "spice" in these poems—EPICS

87. **Jumbles:** FLAME KHAKI EYELID BEFALL
Answer: This simply isn't done!—HALF-BAKED

88. **Jumbles:** RUMMY WAFER FRACAS GARLIC
Answer: It's warm with it—SWARM

89. **Jumbles:** SILKY BURST DEFAME FEMALE
Answer: What he suffered from on a boring date—"LASS-ITUDE"

90. **Jumbles:** ARRAY MOOSE DETAIN BARREN
Answer: What you could find if you just opened the dictionary at random—"RANDOM"

91. **Jumbles:** VILLA SNORT EITHER BOUNCE
Answer: Something new in neckwear—"NOVEL-TIES"

92. **Jumbles:** GROOM HITCH FRIGID RATIFY
Answer: She doesn't like to receive one or look one—A FRIGHT

93. Jumbles: GLEAM HONOR BODILY INWARD
Answer: Might be a sound investment for those who don't get everything—A HEARING AID

94. Jumbles: BRAND FROZE SOLACE AIRWAY
Answer: One used to be this in or at when he enlisted—SWORN

95. Jumbles: BERTH NIPPY MAINLY COLUMN
Answer: Men in port are conspicuous—"PROMINENT"

96. Jumbles: WHINE CRACK SUNDAE HEARSE
Answer: How to cut up in a cab—USE A HACKSAW

97. Jumbles: COUGH HENNA FROLIC BYGONE
Answer: "Again in France?"—"ENCORE"

98. Jumbles: LEECH BLOOM GENTLE EMBALM
Answer: Sounds like a bit of a nut in the Army—COLONEL ("kernel")

99. Jumbles: PATCH SWISH MAGPIE JIGGER
Answer: Several in a flight—STEPS

100. Jumbles: COCOA HASTY PONDER TACKLE
Answer: This drink might put an end to rumors—SCOTCH

101. Jumbles: FAIRY COLON BUNION TEMPER
Answer: For people down there this place could be no finer—"INFERNO"

102. Jumbles: BOGUS FOYER TAWDRY BEFORE
Answer: Sounds like this crook isn't in danger—A SAFE ROBBER

103. Jumbles: FETID GUMBO SUPERB GADFLY
Answer: What shoes often are, after being bought—"SOLED"

104. Jumbles: LOATH AWARD FERRET SCHOOL
Answer: Why a wig can help you to lie about your appearance—IT'S A "FALSE HOOD"

105. Jumbles: FINNY AMUSE LOCATE JUNKET
Answer: Hard on the hands!—NAILS

106. Jumbles: FATAL EATEN INNING MISERY
Answer: When does a woman do all her talking?—IN HER LIFETIME

107. Jumbles: TEMPO ROBOT HINDER TORRID
Answer: Spreads out under a tree—THE ROOT

108. Jumbles: DUCAT PANSY LOUNGE BISHOP
Answer: This material must be checked!—PLAID

109. Jumbles: NOOSE LIBEL HEALTH ANGINA
Answer: They show signs of brilliance—NEON LIGHTS

110. Jumbles: VIPER MADLY OCELOT DINGHY
Answer: What an unemployed film star is—A MOVIE IDLE

111. Jumbles: PEACE CHAFF PYTHON AVOWAL
Answer: This bird has his hat on!—A "CAP-ON"

112. Jumbles: QUEUE KAPOK SQUALL GROTTO
Answer: The extremities one might reach!—TOES

113. Jumbles: KNAVE CEASE INVEST KISMET
Answer: They contain more feet in winter than in summer—ICE SKATES

114. Jumbles: WELSH TACKY AFLOAT SUBDUE
Answer: Sounds like it could be worn in the window—A SASH

115. Jumbles: HOBBY TWILL FLAGON ADDUCE
Answer: A kind of butter that's spelled with four letters—G-O-A-T

116. Jumbles: SPITE KETCH EASILY ABACUS
Answer: Might make you cross at the end of a letter—KISSES

117. Jumbles: EXUDE FAUNA REDUCE GALAXY
Answer: This could make you feel you ought to do something—AN URGE

118. Jumbles: CATCH REARM WORTHY SALUTE
Answer: May help prevent an invasion by air—A SCARECROW

119. Jumbles: TAKEN BANDY STOLID DULCET
Answer: You wouldn't take this sitting down!—A STAND

120. Jumbles: DRONE VOCAL FEALTY INHALE
Answer: It should be put back on its course—A DIVOT

121. Jumbles: GAWKY TARRY NUTRIA DEFINE
Answer: The first part is rather heavy, but the whole can be lifted easily—and willingly!—A "TANK-ARD"

122. Jumbles: LITHE PRIZE BRUTAL CAJOLE
Answer: What shape is a kiss?—ELLIPTICAL ("a lip tickle")

123. Jumbles: OAKEN CLUCK FECUND MISFIT
Answer: Generally comes after cheese—A MOUSE

124. Jumbles: JADED BYLAW BUCKLE HIATUS
Answer: A mopping-up operation by the Navy—SWAB

125. Jumbles: GOUTY TYING MINGLE COMEDY
Answer: Often grows sharper with use—A TONGUE

126. Jumbles: SUMAC PRONE VANITY ATTAIN
Answer: This Russian has four to start with!—IV-AN

127. Jumbles: GLUEY JUMPY ASTHMA RADISH
Answer: "She's a gem and much rarer than the mother of her"—"PEARL"

128. Jumbles: ABOUT WAGER PERMIT KINGLY
Answer: He had some redeeming features—THE PAWNBROKER

129. Jumbles: LEAVE BATON UNLESS ABDUCT
Answer: How to complain about a dull knife—BE BLUNT

130. Jumbles: SURLY GROUP PLOVER ENOUGH
Answer: What the barker's offspring were called—PUPS

131. Jumbles: ARMOR POACH MARKUP SOIREE
Answer: Could be a useless thing—to fight over!—A SCRAP

132. Jumbles: SAHIB GUISE DECENT PLURAL
Answer: This warm liquid can have a melting effect—TEARS

133. Jumbles: CUBIT FOCUS POLITE BEAVER
Answer: There may be objections involved in the use of these words!—"BUTS"

134. Jumbles: THINK SOAPY BEADLE FIDDLE
Answer: "Must be nails in your shoe!"—"TOENAILS"

135. Jumbles: BASSO VOUCH DIVIDE MELODY
Answer: "Dropped" by a nosy person—"EAVES" (eavesdropped)

136. Jumbles: FRAME BARGE NORMAL MURMUR
Answer: You might break into this when in a hurry—A RUN

137. Jumbles: HUMAN TESTY RATION PENCIL
Answer: "Could connect us with that woman!"—"US-HER"

138. Jumbles: MONEY BOUND FOMENT LADING
Answer: "Come out in the garden!"—"BLOOM"

139. Jumbles: FORTY BRAIN MULISH POORLY
Answer: What people who boo at performers sometimes are—"BOO-RS"

140. Jumbles: EMBER PEONY KETTLE BAFFLE
Answer: Sounds like you might take a look at this dog in China—A "PEKE"

141. Jumbles: ESSAY SCARY SHOULD LIMPID
Answer: Divides by uniting and unites by dividing—SCISSORS

142. Jumbles: DUCAL FIFTY MENACE IODINE
Answer: Not to be played with when loaded—DICE

143. Jumbles: LEAKY POISE CHALET PHYSIC
Answer: Far from alert but outwardly sly—"SL-EEP-Y"

144. Jumbles: POKER BASIC UNCURL CORPSE
Answer: A kind of European curtain material—IRON

145. Jumbles: TOKEN HUSKY GIBBET FORGET
Answer: When dropped are meant to be taken up by someone else—HINTS

146. Jumbles: WEDGE TOXIC COMPEL WEAPON
Answer: Dragged away—to get married—"TO-WED"

147. Jumbles: ROBIN TULIP SHADOW VOYAGE
Answer: You wouldn't expect to find her at home!—A VISITOR

148. Jumbles: NEEDY USURP EMERGE INVOKE
Answer: Where an astronomer might find poetry—IN THE "UNI-VERSE"

149. Jumbles: GLADE ELEGY MYRIAD ABRUPT
Answer: What you'll find in the room of your dreams—A BED

150. Jumbles: STEED GAILY AMBUSH CALMLY
Answer: Might be barred in some parks—CAGES

151. Jumbles: BOUGH FLUTE WEAKEN DARING
Answer: You might be powerless to accept this—A TOW

152. Jumbles: PIETY AUDIT HAMMER MALTED
Answer: It's always done in the evening!—THE DAY

153. Jumbles: GLOVE PUTTY MILDEW BROGUE
Answer: How to sell an electrical gadget—PLUG IT

154. Jumbles: RAINY LATHE CLEAVE FEUDAL
Answer: Working he gets all the dirtier—THE CLEANER

155. Jumbles: ENACT DECAY BECAME PATTER
Answer: Taken down inside—EATEN

156. Jumbles: PARCH SKUNK FACILE NEARLY
Answer: What that Portuguese neighbor is—SPAIN

157. Jumbles: BASIN EXACT ABUSED CANDID
Answer: Made a dent in the history of literature—DANTE

158. Jumbles: GIANT DOILY BOILED KNOTTY
Answer: What the billy goat said to his mate—YOU'RE KIDDING!

159. Jumbles: OFTEN SUITE FRUGAL THEORY
Answer: A loud cry that's quiet to start with—"SH-OUT"

160. Jumbles: WHOOP ENSUE DEBATE NUMBER
Answer: How they knew he was the proprietor—HE OWNED UP

161. Jumbles: PALLID ACTING EITHER CAJOLE FECUND COOKIE
Answer: Why he died laughing—HE WAS TICKLED TO DEATH

162. Jumbles: VACANT WEDGED OMELET TETHER RATIFY PENMAN
Answer: Your fare should be reduced if you're this—OVERWEIGHT

163. Jumbles: THIRTY FINISH ABACUS WEAKEN BEAVER PARADE
Answer: What you get when you're kidnapped by a ghost—SPIRITED AWAY

164. Jumbles: CONVOY OFFSET ABUSED FERVID INJURY GIBLET
Answer: "Why is she marrying an officer?"—"HE MADE A GOOD OFFER, SIR!"

165. Jumbles: SMUDGE DAHLIA ACTION KNOTTY FIGURE DROPSY
Answer: Make music—and nonsense!—FIDDLESTICKS!

166. Jumbles: CACTUS HAMMER BRONCO EMBODY SHANTY PEWTER
Answer: Why the jockey called the vet—HIS HORSE WAS SCRATCHED

167. Jumbles: ELEVEN BRUTAL HIDING AMBUSH PUNDIT CANNED
Answer: He blushed right down to his fingertips because he was this—CAUGHT RED-HANDED

168. Jumbles: EMBARK SALOON TUXEDO HINDER LEGACY PHYSIC
Answer: What he was when he found a pearl in the oyster—"SHELL" SHOCKED

169. Jumbles: TURKEY VACUUM OBLIGE IMPUTE UNEASY STOLID
Answer: What the librarian's looks did—SPOKE VOLUMES

170. Jumbles: WALNUT ABDUCT MOHAIR QUAINT GALAXY PARLOR
Answer: You'll be charged after a ride in this—A PATROL WAGON

171. Jumbles: SAVORY DARING BASKET MODIFY VANITY UNLESS
Answer: How much can a freeloader drink?—ANY GIVEN AMOUNT

172. Jumbles: IMMUNE DEBATE PATTER FATHOM QUARRY OBTUSE
Answer: Why the blond would have nothing to do with the hippie—SHE WAS FAIR & SQUARE

173. Jumbles: GASKET INVEST LAVISH CLERGY MATURE FACILE
Answer: Why is a mouse like grass?—THE CAT'LL EAT IT

174. Jumbles: PRISON TRIPLE SALUTE INVOKE MOTIVE ALIGHT
Answer: How to get your clothes off faster than others—OUTSTRIP THEM

175. Jumbles: FIESTA TONGUE BEFORE STYMIE CATCHY POLITE
Answer: You might have a vested interest in this!—A THREE-PIECE SUIT

176. Jumbles: WHENCE BELONG MODISH SUBDUE FOSSIL LOUNGE
Answer: What a good body snatcher wouldn't be without on a night like this—HIS "GHOUL-OSHES"

177. Jumbles: INFLUX PLURAL DENOTE BUCKLE TWINGE AROUND
Answer: This vessel contains just a little more than four quarts—A "GALL-E-ON"

178. Jumbles: WATERY BAFFLE CRAYON VOYAGE TANDEM ENSIGN
Answer: What you wouldn't expect to get from a man of few words—A LONG SENTENCE

179. Jumbles: NIMBLE UNLOAD BUTTON ENABLE KILLER CHOSEN
Answer: What the talkative whale was—A BIG BLUBBERMOUTH

180. Jumbles: ENJOIN HOPPER DISARM BLOUSE ZIGZAG ENTITY
Answer: At a place like this expect them at closing time—PARTING SHOTS